The Crow's Enchanted Dance:

The Phenomenology of Sacred Place and Sacred Space

Dr. K. Mark Hilliard

with Photojournalist
Emily Mae Bergeron

Copyright 2017, by Dr. K. Mark Hilliard
ISBN: 978-0-9966962-9-6

Editors: Rosemary J. Hilliard and Jessa Rose Sexton
Photojournalist: Emily Mae Bergeron
Photographs and Cover Photo: Emily Mae Bergeron
Cover and Book Design: Whitnee Clinard

All rights reserved. No part of this publication may be reproduced or transmitted in any form or by any means without written permission of the author.

Published by
Moloney-O'Brien

A division of The Hilliard Institute
for Educational Wellness and Hilliard Press

Franklin, Tennessee
Abbeyleix, Ireland
Oxford, England

www.hilliardinstitute.com
mark.hilliardinstitute@gmail.com

The Crow's Enchanted Dance:

The Phenomenology of Sacred Place and Sacred Space

Dr. K. Mark Hilliard

with Photojournalist
Emily Mae Bergeron

moloney ⊗ o'brien

Table of Contents

1) The Dance Begins..7
2) In Quest of Authenticity...11
3) The Phenomenology of Mystery, the Imagination, and Enchantment 15
4) Sacred, Spiritual, or Haunted....................................37
5) Sacred as a Religious or Divine/God Term......................41
6) Sacred as a Meta-Physical or Spiritual Term...................47
7) Sacred as a Physiological or Psychological Term..............51
8) The Sacred and History...57
9) The Sacred and the Senses......................................61
10) The Sacred and Ritual: Spirit-Ritual............................77
11) The Sacred and Nature..87
12) Qualities of Sacred Encounters................................95
13) What is Place...101
14) What is Space..105
15) What Is Sacred Place..109
16) What Is Sacred Space...127
17) Sacred Sites: Sacred Places and Sacred Spaces...........141
18) The White Crow's Enchanted Dance........................167
19) Bibliography..170

The Crow's Enchanted Dance

Chapter One
The Dance Begins

It was early morning, the summer of 1996. A summer that was a bit too hot and humid for the typical mountain climate of the Qualla Boundary, a region known by most from outside its borders as the Eastern Band of the Cherokee Indian Reservation. This is a primitive and sacred land deep in the Appalachian Mountains of North Carolina that, unfortunately, many only experience as a tourist town. I had come back to these mountains to reacquaint myself with the Boundary of my youth. A place I had worked alongside my parents during the 1960s. Mom and Dad were missionaries in these mountains when I was a boy, and in my adulthood, I had been drawn back to this enchanted place to live and work on my doctoral dissertation. My research was a study of the traditional teaching and learning styles of the Eastern Band of the Cherokee people.

Little did I know that this time of cultural re-acquaintance and research would extend well beyond my graduate studies, and the lessons learned from my days with the Cherokee would become an essential part of my teaching and learning philosophy far into my academic career. It was during these days, living and working on the Boundary and the surrounding Smoky Mountains, that I begin to write my first book on holistic wellness. And it is the place where, many, many years later, I began working on my seventh book—a story of sacred place and space.

On this June morning, I arose at dawn, something I was not apt to do, and stepped outside to a beautiful smoky blue haze as thick as fog on the surrounding mountains, a phenomenon that gave the name *Smoky* to the Great Smoky Mountains of Tennessee and North Carolina. I was staying in a small house in Wolfe Town, a historic Native community, with Charles and Ruth, a family who had lived on the reservation for many years. Charles was one-quarter Cherokee and a visionary Cherokee teacher and spiritual leader, but his health was now beginning to fail him. He was quickly tumbling into the progressive stages of dementia, and he had asked me to help him continue with his weekly preaching, teaching, and spiritual classes, which were becoming more difficult for him with each passing day. I agreed.

I had been awoken by the vocal-dance of crows outside my window. An enthusiastic choral-ballet of dancing crows. To me, it was a reverberation of ethereal enchantment. A ritualistic melody of the spheres. Of all the sounds of nature, this one seems to call to my heart the most. As I stepped out into the crows' sacred world of outside-*space* composed of God-created grass, soil, and air from my inside-*place* of manmade paneled wood, carpet, and brick, the birds took gentle flight. As they left the ground, it was as if they were waving goodbye with their long and pointed wings. As I recall this moment, the image is like the slow-motion application in film used to emphasize specific moments, allowing the observer to pay particular attention to each frame of moment-movement individually. My eyes were then drawn from the birds, now in air, back to the earth below them. Back to real time and real space, back to an object my winged friends had left behind. A black silk-like stalk

Chapter 1

was protruding from their former dance ground. I walked over and picked up the crow feather. As I held it up, a familiar voice behind me spoke up. "That's a sign for you, you know."

Charles had stepped onto the porch in a brown long sleeved shirt, awkwardly folded back on one arm, with faded jeans that were a bit too baggy and a bit out of place on this man who usually wore a suitcoat and tie, with an old grey hat in his right hand, and a red, black, blue, and white Cherokee beaded medallion, with the symbol of a dream catcher at its center, draped around his long, thin neck. He had been a tall, solid figure of a man just a year earlier, before this disease had begun to take its toll on his body, and in this brief moment I could see that strength once again.

Charles continued to share with me about the extraordinary crow. His words revealed a bit about the bird's history in Cherokee culture. That as a bird, he is a distinctive animal because he both walks on the earth and flies in the heavens. And as a crow, he holds recognition as a messenger between both worlds, a guardian of sacred place and a guide into sacred space, and as such, Charles finished by saying: "The crow knows the thin spots well."

I have come to believe that those who obtain in-depth spiritual wisdom have a tendency to lose a portion of their connectedness to this physical world and its temporal language. So was Charles sharing spiritual wisdom, or words of dementia? Whichever the case, those words, spoken on a specific day in time and space over twenty years ago, take visual form in this book I have titled *The Crow's Enchanted Dance: The Phenomenology of Sacred Place and Sacred Space*. That feather, aging quite respectively, still sits a-top my wooden writing board each day, as if it is a quilled pen shaping each word formed from the pondering thoughts of my spirit, my soul, my mind, and body, as each finger kinesthetically works its action on my keyboard. I hope you join me on this journey of intense research, pondering words, and enchanted memory.

Heritage Park Trail, Spring Hill, Tennessee

Chapter Two
In Quest of Authenticity

In examining a topic like sacred place and sacred space, I find it fitting to begin with some questions of authenticity and then to examine these questions in the research that follows. I also find it beneficial to attempt to leave behind any pre-conceived notions of what sacred places and sacred spaces are. When we think we know what we are looking for, we often overlook reality in search of myth.

The following are some of the questions that drove and continue to drive my research.

- Do sacred places and sacred spaces exist?
- If they exist, are they a corporal reality, a spiritual reality, or only a part of our creative imagination and daydream-type fantasies?

- Are sacred places and spaces a product of emotional and genetic memory, or are they a spiritual phenomenon?
- Are sacred places and sacred spaces the same, or do they represent two separate compositions?
- Do sacred places and sacred spaces always represent a connection to God or a concept of a higher power, or can they also represent a meaningful connection to the physical and psychological?
- Can places and spaces hold a memory of the past to which we can connect, a *storied memory*? **Storied memory** relates to the concept of a memory to tell a story, not simply present a fact or a *stored* memory.
- Can memory be only held in the mind of an individual to re-tell the story, or can it also be stored in matter with which an individual may personally connect and interpret?
- If one believes in a universe created by God, is not all that is created sacred? Is there a difference in that which is sacred, that which is spiritual, and that which is haunted?
- Can sacred places and sacred spaces be created or recreated by an artist, a writer, a musician, an architect, or a designer?
- What makes a place or space sacred?
- Is there a difference between sacred place and sacred space—singular, and sacred places and sacred spaces—plural.
- Are there common physical elements located at sacred places and spaces?
- With what do we connect at a sacred place or space—a power, an entity, an emotion, a presence, a past-presence, God?
- What helps us connect or hinders us from connecting? Why do some people connect and others do not?
- And, does the sacred reside within the place, the space, or the individuals encountering the place or space?

Chapter 2

To begin to understand the theory of sacred place and sacred space and these related questions, it is important to first understand the various meanings behind the three terms *sacred*, *place*, and *space*. It is likewise important to value the fact that individuals approach this subject from a variety of stances. Some approach it from a religious standpoint with God as the divine source of all that is sacred, others from a meta-physical or spiritual standpoint that may or may not involve religion and one's sense of God, and some from more of a physiological or psychological (physio-psycho) point of view with the concept of what we perceive as sacred to be understood within the realm of science and the physical makeup of our world, our mind, and our body. I will attempt to address each of these views in the chapters that follow. But I want to begin with a chapter on the concept of enchantment, mystery, and the imagination as holding key roles in understanding the phenomena of sacred place and sacred space. Without a willingness to explore the world of enchantment that surrounds us everywhere, every day, one will not discover the world of sacred place and space.

Cades Cove, Smoky Mountains National Park

Chapter Three
The Phenomenology of Mystery, the Imagination, and Enchantment

Phenomenology

Phenomenology is the study of phenomena: a philosophical study of unexplained structures of experience. Such a study examines the way we as humans interpret and process events and relationships to and encounters with these events. Phenomena appear to be a structure of both physical and spiritual consciousness—meta-consciousness. Through sensory and meta-sensory awareness, a phenomenon offers the opportunity for individual reception and interpretative meaning for anyone within its perceptive range.

Mystery, the Imagination, and Enchantment

To understand the phenomena of sacred place and sacred space, one must first appreciate the concepts of mystery, the imagination, and enchantment. We must learn how to allow our spirit and soul to come out and play in our everyday world. We do not encounter the sacred without such interplay. Whether in personal research or personal encounters, the sacred is, and always will be, founded on mystery and enchantment as much as it is on fact. This does not imply we are to dismiss fact in the pursuit of mystery, but we must learn to bring these two, often opposing, suppositions into harmony before we can begin to understand anything about the sacred. We must, therefore, gain access to, and make appropriate use of, our imagination, or we will not encounter the sacred. Why? Because the sacred resides outside the physical plane of existence. It is outside the sole realm of cognitive logic and analytical understanding, in the often-unseen world of enchanted reality. Until we can see beyond our self-limiting optical vision, we fall short of the goal of encountering that which is currently beyond that vision, yet well within the potential of an enlightened human encounter.

Mystery

Mystery is that which is yet to be uncovered. It is what lies beyond the façade or covering of earthy matter or human restrained thinking and vision. It is facts to be revealed, as well as secrets that may never be. Mystery entails a transversing of the senses—the magic of tasting a color, smelling the cold, or hearing that which produces no audible sound—all without understanding the why of the phenomena. A true, modern-day mystic is not the clairvoyant psychic of meta-physical novels, but is simply one who searches for this mystery, understanding that it is the excursion, the moment-of-mystery, the delicate and brief touch of enlightenment that brings realization and excitement, even if the mystery itself is never revealed. Mystery is as real and meaningful as that which is clearly discernable. Without it, life is an artless journey of the mundane. Our search for

Chapter 3

sacred place and sacred space brings us into this world of creative mystery and opens windows, doors, and undisclosed passageways into an enchanted world, the sacred world of the spirit, awaiting our entry.

Imagination

Imagination can be a construction of the subconscious or unconscious mind into the conscious, or it can be a flow of the meta-physical or spiritual into the same. If this transfer occurs by the action of spirit, it is the expanded imagination.

What some call the intuitive imagination may indeed offer images and words of wisdom of a truer value than those we create with the analytical mind or the objective imagination. This more dynamic, expanded imagination enriches the faculty of thought to generate beauty and interact with ethereality at an un-paralleled intensity as compared to that of the unrefined imagination.

Expanded Imagination

I depict the merger of mystery and logic in our imagination as the expanded imagination, the meta-imagination, or the spirit-imagination. For cannot the practical and the enchanted co-exist for the same eyes, the same lips, the same mind, the same spirit? This is not the rudimentary imagination of our simple daydreams of fictitious fantasy, but the imagination of enchanted potentiality, the imagination of the human mind as it resonates with the human spirit and the human spirit as it resonates with the Creator and the spiritual essence of the creation. The imagination as it passes beyond simple physical/psychological (physio/psycho) sensory stimulation, to a deeper/higher level of transcendent recognition. That place where the mundane and the sacred share a kiss, and the magic of this romantic union begins to unfurl. This is the imagination of the human spirit inspired by life.

This expanded imagination, if rightfully preserved, involves the freedom of our youthful mind and body of wonderment, entwined with the experience and wisdom offered by the maturity of a life lived. Far too often we naively, or by force, grow out of this wondrous stage of youthful admiration for mystery and enchantment and replace it with a dreary acceptance of the ordinary. With that mindset, that which is sacred remains forever hidden beneath a heavy veil.

In his book, *The Poetics of Space*, French philosopher of the early to mid-twentieth century, Dr. Gaston Bachelard (1994 – originally published in French in 1958) refers to what I call the expanded imagination as "daydreams." Not daydreams of a wondering and simplistic mind, moving from random subjects and images to more random subjects and images, but the daydream of the spirit, transporting our thoughts outside the physical boundaries of mind and matter. Transcendentalist philosopher William Rogers (1947) suggests that subjective and unseen phenomena are too subtle to be received by the gross senses of natural man. They require a super-sensory, intuitive consciousness, a meta-imagination.

In-Spirit and the Expanded Imagination

I have found that it is in our moments *in-spirit* that our expanded imagination rises and overflows into our physical being of mind and body and outward into the world around us. This in-spirit is more than a physical state of being, it is a spiritual, or meta-physical state of being where in we move from physical consciousness to meta-consciousness. In-spirit, we have full access to our expanded imagination of creative possibilities, or perhaps it is in-spirit that the expanded imagination is crafted. Too often, we become the sum of our cognitive collected history; our expanded imagination allows us to explore beyond this impending obstacle into our yet unknown possibilities.

Chapter 3

When we learn to achieve in-spirit, our expanded imagination becomes the place where *beyond our wildest imagination* takes breath. It is a place where we are always elsewhere, yet in our elsewhere, we are always present. In the in-spirit expanded imagination, we can reside within our body while our spirit transcends to other places, other realms. This unique in-spirit aspect of the expanded imagination is not merely something to be contemplated, or a place in which to contemplate. It is an inner experience in need of expression. The expressive words imparted to and by our spirit have a far greater poetic value than the words we use in our everyday thought and conversation. I personally feel compelled to capture these words in an abundance of journals that lie about my house in what appears to be arbitrary fashion, but are indeed systematic in placement within the rooms where my thoughts tend to flow most easily. Within these diaries my now captive-words await a new life in written or illustrated form. I try never to allow entrancing words or phrases to slip away without recording their visual shape for further inquiry and use.

Memory and the Expanded Imagination

Sometimes, distinguishing our memory from our imagination and our imagination from our expanded imagination is difficult. Our memory is never of what is present in the moment, but our interpretation of what was in the past, greatly influenced by a significant number of lifespan variables: the systematic influence of our logical mind; the potency of our spirit-mind—our ability to gain and maintain access to in-spirit; our momentary circumstance in time; our values, beliefs, and expectations; fragments of our upbringing, knowledge, intelligence, education, and experiences; the everchanging flow of chemicals within our mortal body; the angle from which we viewed the objects of our memory; the span of time transpiring between memory-creation and memory-recall; and personal human biases. When anyone tells a story, even his own story, it is influenced by these life-variables. Memory and our imagination tend to merge together in our expressive presentations. For me, that is a bit of the magic, the enchantment. While the imagination, and expanded imagination, might incubus a nightmare when there is a need for exactness of recall, it is a never-never land of enchanted vision for sensory and meta-sensory excitement and creative experience.

As a creative experience, the expanded imagination expresses the poetry of memory and the supernatural state of in-spirit, engaged by reality. It allows us to transcend the common place, to a place of wonder, mystery, and awe. Not a land of fantasy, but an authentic and engaging wonderland of potentiality.

Divine Imagination

The famous Irish poet, author, and priest, John O'Donohue (*Divine Beauty*, 2004) addresses the concept of a "Divine Imagination—the source of our creative longings and passion" (pp. 150-151). As people of the world, we have been encouraged to disregard any potential embrace by the divine. We become satisfied with the gift of intellect, even in our spirituality. But, within the concept of an imagination that connects us with God, we can discover a whole new sense of our world and the imagination of its Creator. "Every tree, bird, star, stone, and wave existed first as a dream in the mind of the divine artist. In-deed the world is a mirror of the divine imagination and to decipher the depths of this world is to give insight into the heart of God. The traces of the divine imagination are everywhere." Through this divine imagination, all things were created and therefore infused with the secret depths of their Maker. The more we learn to share in this imagination, the more we encounter the sacred gifts the creation, and our Maker, bring to light. Yet we continue to entangle our thoughts with this material world of matter and physical cognitive intellect alone, gravely restricting ourselves from our created capabilities.

Dr. Bachelard (1994) rightly communicates that today's world of intellect discourages us from seeking further information about that which seems incidental, insignificant, or contrary to normal or abject thinking. Our expanded imagination goes beyond our self-limiting intellect and gains us access to God's imagination, and there we discover that that which is discouraged, is often found to be of undeniable significance. I do not take Bachelard's interpretation of divine imagination to infer that we as humans have divine imagination, but that within our expanded imagination, we have access to this divine resource and divine inspiration.

Pre-Enchantment

Enchantment lies often dormant within each of us, waiting to be unfolded and released like the shadows of the morning terrain. Each of our senses are programmed with the power to allow this inner-enchantment, this pre-enchantment, to bloom.

The feeling of *enchantment* expresses a position of pre-enchantment—some inner-enchantment potentiality places the emotion recognized as enchantment into play. Something that is, perhaps, comprised of memory (love, romance, care, family, friends, place, space); imagination (the imagination of the human mind and/or the expanded imagination of our human spirit); or the substance of immemorial content (a spirit-memory of our Creator or of our physio-psycho pre-history outside our genetic capabilities) inspires a sensation, prompted by a stimulation (often initiated by a place, space, or object), creating a reaction—enchantment. If this is so, do not we all, as creations *made from and of* God's enchanted power, of God Stuff, have the ability to connect with, or re-connect with, this pre-enchantment through a sacred place or space? Subsequently, if we allow this arousal of pre-enchantment to become enchantment, can it not be experienced and expressed as happiness, joy, or a feeling of inner-conscious connectivity, peace, and awe? These emotions expressed "happily" together under the sensory shelter of enchantment?

As physio-psycho sentiments alone, pre-enchantment is often experienced with very temporal emotions. As enchantment, these emotional reverberations can be experienced for extended periods of time and even in the mist of distress and turmoil. While enchantment is initially an in-the-moment occurrence—that moment of magic when the unexpected occurs—once allowed to grow and flourish, those moments become more frequent, and more prolonged, and enchantment becomes a way of life. An even more impressive potentiality of this co-habital arrangement is that we can essentially lessen the amount of distress and turmoil we allow into our lives by acceding more moments to pre-enchantment, by allowing more moments for enchantment to take its appropriate place in our daily lives. Sacred places and sacred spaces provide both visual and articulate venues for this occurrence. They encourage communication at the level of spiritual essence. They allow our human spirit to communicate with the spiritual nature residing in a place or space. They allow us to communicate with God.

Enchantment

Is enchantment a mere youthful entranced folly, an imaginative charm without an extensive ancestry, or can we distinguish between enchanted folly and meta-physical actuality? Is there true substance, a presence of existence, in our enchanted experiences, or are they a reckless abandonment of reality? To me, the meta-physical actuality of enchantment is not some whimsical emotion of mysticism, but it embodies the totality of all things possessing actuality, including those things that can be explained and those that cannot. Enchantment denotes the place and space where the physical joins with the spiritual of an actual experience and symbolizes the science and mystery of people, places, spaces, and things. Enchantment occurs as a cognitive/meta-cognitive and physical/meta-physical expressive actuality. Even the word itself, *enchantment*, possesses an inner, intimate, sacred conviction of how life is intended to be lived. It is a word to be both shouted and whispered. It is a sacred word. If not, enchantment is merely a daydreaming state of fanciful make-believe.

Enchantment is our beyond-magical capacity for meta-sensory engagement. It is authentic-magic. It is a sacred encounter, a prayer answered before it is prayed. Enchantment offers an exquisite agitation of the senses with both brief and extended moments of the purest delight. It is pure love bursting forth from her very host, to be shared with her guests. Enchantment is a gift I request and acquire every day. I value it as greatly as wisdom—even more-so than pretentious earthly wisdom. I envision enchantment as the most beautiful of brides. She presents herself in all her inner beauty when she is needed the most. She captures our heart, and holds it tightly. We fall in love, and remain in love, with all she represents. We wish to experience her presence every day and pursue her countless endowments with all our might.

Some believe that to reminisce offers enchantment, but to me to reminisce only offers a sweet vapor of our exhausted past. Yes, there is fleeting pleasure to be aroused through the art of our moments of evocative memory. But, what are we to do when their feathered touch fades beyond our reach, that place where our memory is ever-so spoiled with yesterday's sadness. I am not, per-say, against reminiscing of the past, but, its rightful place is to move us toward the enchantment awaiting us today. Abandoned reminiscing is of the past. Devoted enchantment is of today. I embrace enchantment as the better bequest. Enfold her with all your strength.

If you have ever been enchanted, if you have ever experienced enchantment's gratifying gift, you have encountered that which is sacred, that which is otherworldly, that which is sanctified for blessed intent. With enchantment, we take hold of the wind with the arms of our soul and place it in the heart of our spirit. Enchantment is so much more than a psychological emotion to be felt. It is a meta-emotion of the spirit. It is an attraction, an allure, a manifested sense of awe created by an ethereal presence that is beyond any other sensory experience we can possibly know. Yet, this gift of enchantment is seldom encountered by those within whose grasp it is so easily procured. In our everyday walk of work and play it is there.

So effortless is its magical presence that a child perceives it with pleasure, a smile, or a laugh; yet adults amble pass with little notice of its invitation, or even of its very existence. It is a presence absent to the lower enslaved senses, but very much alive and unshackled to the higher ones. In the words of Christ, we are to "become as children." As such, we accept enchantment's welcome gift to enter the realm of the heavenly (Matthew 18:3, New American Standard Bible).

Triggers for Enchantment

Over the twenty years of my study of sacred place and sacred space, I have gathered a collection of sensory stimulation triggers that individuals have shared as prompts for their experiences with enchantment. I share these by category.

- **Passageways:** gateways, open gates, bridges, windows, doors (especially open doors, pathways, trails, stairs).
- **Holy Ground:** cemeteries, burial grounds, burial mounds, the Holy Lands where Jesus walked, and other religious land/grounds, and the simple act of walking on the natural earth as compared to pavement or other man-made pathway coverings.
- **Natural Sounds:** mourning doves, song birds, crows, night sounds (crickets, frogs), running water like creeks and rivers, waterfalls, wind, rain, storms, thunder, the ocean waves.
- **Natural Smells:** berries, flowers, trees in bloom, herbs, earth and soil, cut grass and hay, rain.
- **Water Forms:** mist, fog, clouds, waterways or bodies of water (creeks, rivers, lakes, streams), snow, waterfalls, rainbows.
- **Natural Light:** fire, candles, sunlight, moonlight, sun through stained glass windows, shadows.

- **Life Forms:** animal life (especially birds in flight like doves or flocks of geese), plant life (especially trees), small life forms like fireflies, dragonflies, butterflies, ladybugs.

- **Love and Family Celebrations:** family holidays, birthdays, anniversaries, Valentine's Day, Christmas, weddings, dating, marriage.

- **Miniature Forms:** small scale models of large scale items like trains; villages; children; baby animals like kittens, puppies, rabbits; miniature breeds of animals like miniature goats and horses.

- **Hand-Made or Hand-Grown Items for Consumption:** cigars, wine, spirits, tea, coffee, and the containers we drink from like hand cut crystal or bone China.

- **Hand-Made Items to Wear or with which to Accessorize:** clothing, pocket squares, scarves, leather goods, hats.

- **Expressive Emotions:** laughter, tears, smiles, a kiss, a hug, holding hands and other intimate touch, playfulness, and other sensory expressions of love.

- **Broad Sweeping Vistas or Views:** open fields, rolling hills, mountains, hilltops, oceans, landscapes—plus the boundaries that surround any open spaces like cemeteries or open fields.

- **Dim or Low Light:** candles, sunsets, sunrises, dawn or morning, dusk or evening.

- **Changing Seasons:** especially spring and fall, but even the warmth of summer and the cool air of winter; wind, snow, rain, sun, cold, warmth—each of these provide opportunities for enchanting activities.

- **Elaborate and Simplistic Dwellings:** cathedrals, castles, churches, homes, ruins, abandoned buildings, caves, cottages, lodges.

- **Royalty:** princes, princesses, kings, queens, lords, ladies, dukes, duchesses, and those who serve them such as butlers, footmen, and handmaidens.
- **Round Forms:** circles, domes, mounds, crop circles, passage tombs, round towers, round houses, ringforts, fairy forts.
- **Art Forms:** paintings, drawings, illustrations, sketches, photographs, words, books, poetry, symbols, dance, design.
- **Fancy Dress:** formal dress such as tuxedos, black tie, white tie, cocktail dress or evening gowns; regalia; themed costume and party dress; period dress.
- **Vertical Forms:** crosses, high crosses, steeples, standing stones, round towers.
- **Fantasy:** faeries, fairy tales, dragons, elves, mermaids, leprechauns, unicorns, myth and legend, science fiction, novels.
- **Quietness:** silence, solitude, mystery, alone time (especially time away in nature)
- **Things of Beauty and Soft Sensual Qualities:** lace, cotton, silk, the human form.
- **Nostalgic Forms of Transportation:** trains, boats, carriages, streetcars, trollies, horses, walking.

Biblical Enchantment and Visions

If seeking for Biblical authentication for the enchanted, one has to look no further than the Psalms and Isaiah, where the earth rejoices; fields and all that is within them dance for joy; trees and rivers clap their hands; mountains, hills, and woodlands sing; and beautiful plants grow up from the stems of briers (Psalms 96:11, Psalms 98:8, Isaiah 55:12). Or in Paul's letter to the Romans (Romans 8:21), where the whole creation moans as it longs for renewal. It is not that these characters of nature, in factual and visual deed, perform this magical ballet for all to observe, but if the human spirit allows them to do so in the expanded imagination of both man and creation, the mind concurs and the hearts and souls of man and creation bilaterally rejoice. This rejoicing may be witnessed by all our senses. It is poetry come to life, not simply a poetic metaphor.

This act of enchantment in nature as described by the Psalms—poetry coming to life—is neither to be perceived as literal nor figurative. Literal is much too corpo-real of a definition and figurative is much too un-real. Nature's enchantment is not an artless corporal illustration, nor an illusory sketch. Both dimensional extremes confine enchantment in its authentic power, beauty, and flow. Rather, enchantment in nature is real, in an otherworldly reality. Nature expresses emotions every bit as genuine as human emotions, so we use human emotion terminology in our attempts to explain the real passion experienced and expressed by nature. Yet, nature's enchantment is more ethereal than explanatorily-real. It is beyond real as it relates to physical matter alone, but very real as it relates to the sacred. Enchantment is a product of the union of the real and the ethereal, the physical as it joins with the non-physical, the mundane as it links with the extraordinary. In essence, a third reality is created when this alliance occurs. In the realm of the enchanted, nothing is dictated by conventional terminology or traditional protocol. Predication and assignment are best left among the ordinary aspects of life. They have no place among the enchanted or the sacred.

Synopsis: The expanded imagination of man connects with the expanded imagination of creation and with the Creator. This energy can then be experienced as an emotion of extra-sensory sensation. It may become an image presented within the mind alone, or even an image presented before the optical vision—a visual of what appears to be material form, or the materialization of an otherwise invisible form. An image within, becomes an image without. I'm not talking about an illusion, but rather a vision—the material realm's attempt to discern the non-physical realm through visual interpretation and sometimes visual presentation. If an otherwise lucid mind observes a visual that is not in actuality present, it is likely an enchanted reality of the expanded imagination. It is a real, meta-physical experience. While the trees cannot literally clap non-existent hands, that becomes your authentic translation of personal experience, as you encounter their emotional expression of delight for the rain, the sun, or any other blessing they wish to articulate through joyful expression. Likewise, you might experience nature's painful expressions, as the creation moans for attention and renewal.

Angels Before Us

Our visions of angels may arise from storied memory within a place or space, be granted as a gift within our inspired dreams or visions, exist as the formation of molecular energy shifted into visual images in the atmosphere, or they may stand before us as tangible spirit-beings placed here by God.

My cognitive imagination likes to picture angels as beautiful winged beings of feminine design. But, if I have been visited by angels (and I believe I have) they were adored as ordinary human beings, and presented themselves in both male and female forms. These angelic beings come unannounced at times of need, times for testing of our faith, and times when life's burdens seem too heavy to bear.

With any authentic vision of angels, we need to understand that they are definite spirit-beings created by God, and called to be messengers and ministering servants of God, to mankind. They are real, and if they stand before us it is with purpose and intent. While holy angels follow the directives of their Creator-God, there are also fallen angels who follow their own will and the will or directives of the anti-God—Satan. We should apprise ourselves of whom we entertain (Psalm 91:11, Matthew 4:11, Hebrews 1:14).

We, as humans, are not angels-in-training awaiting our physical death to adorn ourselves with wings of heaven. Yet, we are spirit-beings on this earth, living our lives of spirit and soul within human bodies, as we await the loss of this physical shell, so that we can be transformed into a new, spiritually eternal creation.

In describing angels, various Biblical texts share the following:

- They are like the whisper of spirit brushing closely pass the face, making the hairs of the body stand on end (Job 4:15).
- They have no physical body, but may take on the temporary form of humans in best fulfilling their service to mankind (Genesis 18:1-2, Luke 24:4, Hebrews 13:10).
- They may present themselves as strangers in human form (Hebrews 13:2).
- They may also present themselves in spirit-form (Job 4:16, Matthew 16:27, John 20:11-12, Hebrews 1:14, and throughout the books of Judges and Revelation).
- Their voices may be heard audibly (John 20:13, Revelation 5:11).
- They praise God (Psalm 148:1-5).
- They are not God, nor are they human, but they were created by God—humans are not to worship them (Psalm 148:5, Colossians 2:18, Revelation 19:10).
- They are capable of obeying or disobeying God (Hebrews 1:6, II Peter 2:4).
- They accomplish things individually and in assembly with other angels (Hebrews 12:22).
- They have personality, emotion, purpose, knowledge, and power (Matthew 8:29, Luke 2:13, II Corinthians 11:3).
- They guard and protect mankind (Psalm 91:4, Luke 4:10).
- They may bring answers to prayer (Acts 12:5-10).
- They are observers of God's work on earth (I Corinthians 4:9).

- There are brief proclamations of angels' ability to fly (Revelation 14:6) and in the description of winged cherubim (Ezekiel 1:6 & Exodus 25:20), and the description of winged seraphim (Isaiah 6:2-7).

As spirit-beings not of this earth, angels are not dictated or limited by place and space as we humans are, and angels may, therefore, visit mankind at any time. These visits likely occur more often than we are aware. We are simply not apprised of their call because the ears of our spirit are not attuned.

Of Faeries and Fireflies

Oh, what will the sleep-faeries hold above my closed-lid eyes as I lay my head upon my feathered pillow and dream of another place? Is it a place I can only enter in my dreams, or are my dreams of such lands and fae, shadows of what I may encounter by light?

For several years as a behavioral science professor I oversaw a college research academy in which myself and a group of college students would visit sacred sites and interview individuals regarding their firsthand experiences with personal sacred sites. One of the recurrent encounters shared with us was about unusual visual and auditory experiences. The sites for these experiences were most often very intimate ancestral places such as family farms, woodland, and fields; family cemeteries; and family homes and gardens. A common theme with each account was the lively sound of animals that were not present and visuals of dancing light-forms which seemed to take various, almost lifelike shapes. Some described their image experiences as faeries, little people, or faerie-like. The consistency of these accounts compelled me to add a bit of research to my work on sacred place and space about this phenomenon, which I might formally have dismissed as tales of fantasy.

Chapter 3

The purpose then for incorporating the concept of faeries, or faerie-like visuals, in this section of my text is to encourage readers to move outside personal *ego boundaries*—boundaries of self-limitation by the conscious mind—and move into a state of expanded imagination. This is the same way we experience sacred space—outside our ego boundaries. It, therefore, seems an appropriate way to examine any other unexplainable phenomena.

Ego boundaries is a phrase coined by Dr. Paul Federn and used by Dr. Scott Peck in *The Road Less Traveled* (1978). Examining a phenomenon such as individual encounters with unexplainable sounds and visuals they identify as faeries, or faerie-like images of dancing light, requests an examination of what truly occurs during these personal observations or confrontations. This analysis requires researchers and readers alike to step outside self-imposed ego boundaries and examine experience without bias. Any phenomenon outside our level of conscious-comfort requires us to move beyond these restraints. This section on faeries is not an attempt to confirm or deny the experiences of those interviewed, but more an attempt to understand their experiences through a phenomenological approach. *They saw something; they felt something. Why? What?*

Can the phenomenological image of faeries be real; can they be real for one individual, but not real for another; or are they unreal and simply an illusion of the imagination? Additionally, why do images of faeries charm people so, and is there a value in their enchanting image?

The process of contemplating the concept of faeries, tales of faeries, and faerie-tales, shifts our thinking outside our cognitive limitations into the bigger world of mystery and enchantment. In my research, faeries are not meant to be perceived as a primitive maleficent tribe of magical little people; as spirit-people coming to earth in bodily form from an outer world; as angelic beings; as sub-human beings; nor merely as a product of pretentious illusion. They seem to be more an artifact of man and nature coming together to tell a story through expression. Visuals of faeries, or dancing faerie-type lights, are to be understood in the same sense as trees and rivers clapping their hands; mountains, hills, and woodlands singing; and fields and all that is within them dancing for joy. They are nature's gift of emotional self-expression and expanded imagination, coming in contact with man's gift of self-expression and expanded imagination, creating a visual energy image.

Near the end of my third trip to Ireland, a one-month travel education course with eighteen of my college students, we were hiking on the most mystical trail I have every hiked. We were in the Slieve Bloom Mountains, County Laois, Ireland. The sunlight, in the tall thin trees. The moss inching its way from the ground up the base of each tree. The intermingled sound of nature's primal movements and hypnotic silence. It was magical. Not like a magic show with sleight of hand or even like Disney Land with its wondrous and enchanting props and theatrics. But more a meta-physical magic that I cannot describe with simple words of cognitive sensory expression. There was a highly enhanced sensual presence in the air beyond the ability of the psychological imagination to create. It was the articulation of my surroundings with my expanded imagination. An enchantment that reaches into the heart of the spirit and soul. Pricking and tugging with a dash of excitement, a hint of mystery, and just a touch of fear. Not a negative fear, mind you, but more of a fearful respect of something very unknown and unexplainable. If I had ever been at a place where faeries live as genuine as fireflies, this was it. A place of forest and field where tiny winged creatures, seldom seen with human eyes, might just be experienced with human hearts.

This story of my experience in Ireland does not mean that faeries exist, or that they do not exist, it simply offers the potential for faeries or faerie-like images to *exist* and be witnessed in some auditory or visual manner—or any other similar optical-vision of beyond-tangible-matter to be experienced. The application of the same expanded imagination understanding used for sacred place and sacred space can be used for non-matter optical vision, allowing for

Chapter 3

experiences to exist as more than an illusion or a simple perception for cognitive consideration only, to an image that has a tangible presence. Authentic and academic pursuits should always allow for such a blending of our creative processes as much so as our rational. Otherwise, academia no longer serves its purpose for the advancement of newly revealed authentic truth and understanding. As we examine reality, we must also look to the potentiality of beyond-reality, for reality is simply what we see at one given moment in time. Applying this concept to a potential presence becoming visual within a particular place and space, is about bringing that which is mysterious into our own personal-dimensional reality. That which has spiritual essence, especially elements within nature, is made manifest to our mind and spirit, and sometimes to our optical vision. Is it, therefore, a naive hallucination if we envision mystery laid out before our very eyes? I prefer to address this as unimpaired imagism—isolating a single image to reveal its essence as material reality. We, as humans, do it often with our art, our music, and our poetic words. Cannot nature do it with her art, music, and words as well? Cannot the human spirit do it likewise? What makes us think not? Only our pretentious minds.

Of Faerie Tales and Sacred Space

The ability to picture an unusual or unordinary energy form in nature is a gift of the expanded imagination, allowing us to observe images not visible to the natural eye, but which have a story to tell—A Faerie Tale, if you like. Faerie tales are our attempts to put a story from nature into real words, and in the process a unique language of mystical fantasy, mixed with factual detail, is born. It is neither a literal interpretation or tale, nor a figurative one, but a phenomenon of ethereality. A faerie tale takes place in a meta-physical or sacred space, the only place where it can truly be interpreted and experienced. When I read, or hear a story of faerie and fae, myth and legend, it is now with a new cognition, not my natural cognition, but the meta-cognition.

To experience unexplainable auditory sounds or visual images within our family garden at night is more than a valueless illusion, it is our youthful freedom of wonderment, entwined with our life of experience. It is holding tight to our wondrous stage of youthful admiration for mystery and enchantment. It is never agreeing to replace wonderment for a dreary acceptance of the ordinary. And it is the creation of intimate relationships with nature so that she continually amazes us with her expressions of emotion. Just because something fails to fit our ability to cognitively understand it, just because something appears before our optical vision without clear comprehension, does not mean it is not there. It has a story to tell, an image to share, if we but listen and look. It may be nature, or it may be meta-nature, but it seems to be something frequently experienced by those enchanted by mystery.

Conclusion:
Mystery, the Expanded Imagination, and Enchantment

We are so bombarded with such a daily sensory overload brought on by our physical world that we have disconnected with that which can truly enchant us. This overload blocks our spirit's quest for mystery and enchantment. It is only through an appropriate use of the imagination that we can re-encounter such a reality. This is not the fundamental physio-psycho imagination, but the meta-imagination of the spirit, which, unlike its counterpart, can envision the potential reality that occurs on a spiritual plane always. This then allows the mystery and enchantment projected by a sacred place or space to be received and accepted by the spirit's counterpart, the mind. Thus, the allure and insight into sacred place and sacred space brought on by a blending of factual information such as history and memory, and a more anonymous attraction created by mystery, enchantment, and the expanded imagination.

Aoife's Window, Rock of Dunamase, County Laois, Ireland

Chapter Four
Sacred, Spiritual, or Haunted

The Sacred

That which is sacred is special, unique, personal, honorable, consecrated, or holy. Sacred implies a positive purpose and is something you don't try to change or conform to the norm. It is sanctified, consecrated, or set apart and, therefore, to be respected—even if not understood. In fact, that which is sacred is not meant to be understood as we understand customary knowledge and practices, but it is to be studied and revered with a higher knowledge that is anything but standard. For something to become sacred, it must hold a benefit for humankind and/or its created support system of life—the earth, the sky, the world—the creation.

The Spiritual

Most people relate that which is sacred with that which is spiritual. That which is spiritual is "of the spirit." In practical terms, it is derived from two somewhat opposing words—spirit and ritual. But when combined into their holy wordform, spirit-ritual, the complex significance of that which is spiritual can be observed through ritual, or activity, that involves the spirit (ritual or activity that connects our spirit with our mind, our soul with our body, and our spirit, soul, mind and body with both the physical and spiritual realms of existence). This "of the spirit" can be the spirit of mankind, or the spiritual essence of nature as God's creation. It can also involve spiritual entities and energies that are not of nature or mankind—supernatural entities that never had physical life, and spiritual entities that once had physical life but have that life no longer—past living entities that have died. While the term *spiritual* archetypically carries a positive definition, it can also be used as a negative term involving spiritual evil and death.

Other defining aspects of spiritual include

- an inner, non-genetic sense of uniqueness, creativity, individuality, intuitiveness, and eternal existence;
- knowledge and skills based on an extrasensory sense of things;
- that which is beyond our physical level of understanding;
- the inward components of anything that contains life—spirit, soul, or spiritual essence;
- that which is non-measurable—spirit and soul—over which is formed a physical cloak of existence that is measurable—mind and body; and/or
- our meta-physical stability, our meta-matter.

As opposed to our natural cognition—a product of genetics, study, research, experience, history, and belief—our spiritual cognition is inherent within our spirit and soul and grows and expands as our relationship with God, self, and our world develops.

Chapter 4

Sacred Vs. Spiritual

Is everything that is spiritual, sacred, and is all that is sacred, spiritual? My response to this question did not come until toward the end of this study. My findings? A spiritual thread runs through all that is sacred. The sacred, therefore, must have a spiritual component in order to be sacred. This spiritual component for the sacred might first be observed as a physical or psychological stimulation, but it has the action of a spiritual energy source behind it. The spiritual, on the other hand, may or may not be sacred. Sacred implies a positive force, a higher purpose. Something on the level of the spiritual may or may not have this positive force or higher purpose. The spiritual thread that runs through life can transport both evil and positive spiritual energy. Spiritual energy that is evil, or negative, is not sacred. The use of the spirit for unworthy purposes is not sacred. Sacred places and spaces, therefore, are not the same as haunted places and spaces, based on the definition of *haunted* as negative spiritual energy. This does not preclude the possibility and probability that sacred sites can present spiritual entities; it simply implies that at a sacred site, these entities are positive. It, likewise, does not preclude the possibility that haunted places and spaces can become sacred places and spaces through consecrated efforts.

Cades Cove Methodist Church, Smoky Mountains National Park

Chapter Five
Sacred as a Religious or Divine/God Term

From a religious or divine perspective, that which is sacred involves the heavenly, the holy, the saintly, and the Godly, rather than the physical, the mundane, the genetic, or the earthly. "Sacred space is to celebrate God first, and only then to provide nourishment for the worshiper" (Michael Tavinor, in North & North, 2007, p.31, an Anglican Priest and Dean of Hereford Cathedral, England). Within this category, the purpose for the sacred is to encounter God. The sacred requires human interaction with the divine, in order to exist. On a practical level this interaction entails any of the following three relationships with the divine: that which is *of God*; that which is *from God*; or that which is *set apart for God* (God being defined as the Creator of all that is).

- Of God – the fruit of God's Spirit (joy, peace, love, forgiveness, patience, kindness, goodness, faithfulness, etc.)–qualities *of*

God bestowed upon man, or other elements of creation, as an outgrowth of God or God's Spirit residing within (Galatians, Ephesians). These characteristics are not a common product of man's genetic, survivalistic, natural instinct but are acquired as man and creation become reacquainted and reconnected with their Creator.

- From God – gifts *from God* (the created world, life, breath, food, family, friends)—creation and the things God gives the created world to sustain it and show His love for it.
- Set apart for God – anything we wish to dedicate to God, or that He has dedicated (our lives, our money, our family, an activity, a day, a place, or a space).

At this divine level of the sacred, it may be said that all that is created by God is sacred because it is *of God*, it is made up of *God Stuff*. He spoke, He breathed, He said, He asked, He commanded, and *it was so* (Genesis 1:1-31). God, as the Creator, is not to be viewed as a sleight of hand magician, creating illusions from nothing, anymore than an artist's painting or sculpture would be deemed deceptive magic. Rather, God created and creates everything from Himself, from His actual energy and existence. God's creation is His poem, His song, His story, His painting. God is the original artist of all that we observe as nature. If nature fulfills its sacred vocation, as we encounter it, *in-spirit*, as well as *with-mind*, we become a primordial part of its elements and are enchantedly sustained by it's sensory and meta-sensory comforts. Within the science and mystery of nature, we experience God and our souls are nourished.

In the Biblical text of I Timothy 5: 4-5, the apostle Paul writes to Timothy, one who was given the charge of caring for the church in Ephesus, stating, "Everything created by God is good and nothing is to be rejected if it is received with gratitude; for it is sanctified [sacred] by means of the word of God and prayer" (New American Standard Bible). Thomas Aquinas expressed this conviction of all things beginning from an original divine source as "First Cause." All things have a cause—something that put it into motion, into play—except First Cause (God), which started it all. Aquinas also believed that God and His sacred nature exists in everything before time, and throughout time—by His power, His presence, and His essence (Bourke, 1968).

Sister Benedicta Ward, a friend; a sister of the community of Sisters of the Love of God in Oxford, England; and Reader in the History of Christian Spirituality at the University of Oxford believes the problem in recognizing the sacred is that "we often put a cover over the sacred and change its appearance, even change its complexity, but we do not, we cannot, remove God in the process. He is still there waiting to be uncovered, to be revealed" (personal interview, Benedicta Ward, 2010). She continues her thoughts that "God is everywhere—within each place and within each space between places. When we do not connect with God, it is because we are not ready, we are not prepared, we are trying too hard, we are not open, we are too busy, we are too loud, or we are preoccupied. We need silence and stillness in the place and silence and stillness within ourselves, if we are to connect with the sacred and with God" (personal interview, Benedicta Ward, 2010). Within this pattern of thought it can well be conceived that all that was created has spirit or spiritual essence because it all began *with*, *of*, and *from God*, who is Spirit. This is not a concept we can simply teach with words. We can provide information and we can provide opportunities for experiences to occur, but it is up to the student, the individual, the seeker, to be still and connect with that which is sacred (personal interview, Benedicta Ward, 2010).

My use of the term religion alongside the word divine for this category is more a matter of individual identification as a commonly accepted "God term." It is not, however, the best term to describe man's need for a relationship with God, for the word religion is only included in Biblical text translations a few times. Unfortunately, the concept of religion today and perhaps for a long time, has been misdirected to portray an institutionalized form of spiritual or social activity that has too often conformed to nothing more than a physiological methodology. The term *religion* as seen in its most common form today is not, in-fact, the best way to interpret a divine God. But, the original meaning for the term *religion*, as noted in one of those few Biblical scripts is, indeed, a sacred and authentic calling: "pure and undefiled religion in the sight of our God and Father is this: to visit orphans and widows in their distress, and to keep oneself unstained by the world" (James 1:27, New American Standard Bible). This description denotes God as working through man to accomplish His divine and sacred purposes—meeting the needs of others and not allowing the physical world to control us. He interjects humankind with abilities that we cannot obtain of our own merit. This is true religion and an acceptable account of the role of religion for modern man.

A larger umbrella than the term *religion* under which all that is sacred corresponds are the words *meta-physical* and *spiritual*. If humankind has a spirit and a soul, I use the word spiritual to include both, it makes sense that we can connect with and exhibit these entities through a variety of human applications—religion; art; music; writing; in our attempt to find meaning and purpose in life and work; in sharing ourselves (our gifts and talents) with others; in our dedication of self, a place, or a space; and in experiencing nature and interacting with the creation. Through these types of application, we encounter the sacred, we experience the divine, we get to know God, and we confront true religion, as opposed to the pseudo form of religion that is so prevalent today.

Chapter 5

Mt Hope Cemetery, Franklin, Tennessee

Chapter Six
Sacred as a Meta-Physical or Spiritual Term

The term *meta-physical* tends to be a word used by those who do not organizationally consider themselves religious or tied to a specific religious group, but it does not contradict the existence of God, nor does it argue against the existence of God. Similar wording to meta-physical is used throughout ancient Biblical and non-Biblical texts in reference to other-realms, the un-earthly, the non-physical, the super-natural, the heavenly, and the ethereal.

That which is meta-physically or spiritually sacred is on the level of the mystical, the unexplainable, the extraordinary rather than the natural, the logical, or the ordinary. It cannot be described or understood with commonplace words or activities, nor can it be appreciated with the routine mental processes of the mind apart from the spirit. "Sacred places and spaces are full of history and people's emotional attachments to, or memories of, them. Perhaps sacredness lies not in the actual places, buildings, or locations, but in the hearts and spirits of the people who visit these sites" (Martha Corley, Sacred Place—Sacred Space Class, 2010). In his journal entry on July 16th, 1851, Naturalist, poet, and philosopher Henry David Thoreau wrote, "What temple what fane what sacred place can there be but the innermost part of my own being" (Henry David Thoreau, 1851, in Young, 2009).

These thoughts are not to imply that the sacred lies only within the individual (within the spirit and soul of man), but at the level of the meta-physical, the sacred is a combination of the sacredness of the inner spirit and soul of mankind and a connectivity of this essence with the spiritual or sacred component of all that was created by God. Conceivably, this sacredicity can extend to that which is also created by man—does mankind have the ability to insert individual spiritual essence into something we make or into that with which we have intimate contact? Within this category, the purpose of the sacred is for mankind to interact with the realm of the spirit—with his own spirit and the spirit of creation.

That which is sacred on this level often involves something that is set apart for a higher purpose that may, on the surface, have a physical objective, but this physical objective has spiritual significance. This level of the sacred may or may not specifically relate to one's concept or understanding of God or the divine, but it does relate to the concept of spirit or inner essence—that inner place from which we create a personal drive to seek out meaning and purpose through meta-physical or spiritual thought and action. This higher purpose could be to make the world a better place through spiritual activity, like caring for the needs of our family and others we love. It may involve the use of spirit-rituals to connect, or help others connect, spiritually—praying, singing, playing music, meditating, or using various holy implements or sacraments in these worshipful activities. These methodologies may also be used for sacred religious or divine activities. This higher purpose may also direct us in finding a personal spiritual or sacred place, or by visiting and connecting

Chapter 6

with recognized sacred places and spaces to uncover their mystery. The seeker, however, may or may not be aware of the spiritual motivation behind such action or places for action.

How ever one choses to examine and define the meta-physically sacred, it will always remain full of mystery. If we overlook the mystery and only see the obvious (the observable facts—or what we perceive to be apparent), we can miss much of what is there to greet us, to charm us, to enchant us, and ultimately to enlighten us. This level of the sacred allows us to, at least for a moment, be transported beyond the physical limits of time and space. Though most have experienced this phenomenon at some time, our question often remains: was the spirit, the soul, the mind, or the body actually transported beyond the level of the physical or was it, is it, more a state of emotional transcendence or metaphor? If that which is sacred merely transports our mind and body from its ordinary thoughts and actions, to higher levels of thinking and responses, but still within the confines of our self-limiting physical mind and body, this level of the sacred is merely physiological or psychological. But, if our spirit and soul can reside within our mind and body and at the same time be transported to a higher, non-physical plane, it is a meta-physical, spiritual, or divine phenomenon.

Cades Cove Methodist Church, Smoky Mountains National Park

Chapter Seven
Sacred as a Physiological or Psychological Term

That which is sacred on the level of the physical or psychological has the ability to draw us in, to entice us, to touch us through elements of a physical nature. This physical or psychological impression of the sacred is one that creates emotions, a sense of awe, and elevated levels of multi-sensory stimulation. The stimulation often begins at the level of the mind or the body, but by those approaching it from a religious, divine, meta-physical, or spiritual standpoint, this physical stimulation is meant to move us toward a higher level of thinking and being to that which is spiritual or sacred—nature, stained glass windows, sacred or inspiring music, poetry, art, a special place, an unusual space, the design of a building, or a meaningful historic site to stimulate the physical, then the spiritual. Within this perspective, these physical and psychological elements can *put us in the mood* for spiritual or sacred activity to take place. They generate a spirit-set rather than a mind-set. The inspiration may begin as a physio/psycho emotional encounter, but they then move us to a meta-emotional connection. The Cherokee referred to this staging process as pre-ceremonial ritual, or pre-ceremonial preparation, that may or may not be entered consciously. Sometimes we set the stage for meta-physical activity to occur. At other times, it simply *happens to us*, unexpectedly.

If you are one who participates in church style worship, think of this example: you are stressed from a busy week. It is Sunday morning; you get out of bed late; you awaken the children; you diligently work to get them fed, clothed, in a good mood, and ready to leave for church service. You are now running late, but finally arrive at the church. You hastily unbuckle the children's seat belts, and rush into the building. You are in a mind-set of exhaustion and bad humor. Are you physically and mentally prepared to worship? No. Are there physical elements of the site, the building, the landscape, the atmosphere that can help prepare you to switch gears from your physical thinking, to spiritual thinking? There should be. Is there splendor in the simplicity of design (an old historic church with wooden pews, a mountainside auditorium of nothing more than stones, trees, and earth upon which to sit) or magnificence in the architectural beauty of design (a grand cathedral, stained glass windows exploding with sunlight, color choices that set a psychological and even a spiritual mood) that assists with this physical to meta-physical transition? The fact is, we need there to be such design. While neither a specific place or space, nor a specific design, is spiritually required, and is not of itself to be worshiped, or *overly* valued or praised, distinctive places and designs do provide a great advantage in preparing our spirit, our soul, our mind, and our body for something sacred to occur.

One of the most common understandings of this physio-psycho level of the sacred, is that various elements of physical existence can store memory—a piece of furniture, a building, a grave site, or a place in history where something significant has taken place, etc. As we encounter the element(s), we have the opportunity to encounter

Chapter 7

the memory. This memory may simply be a product of cognitive recall: "When something is sacred it holds special meaning for you, like a garden that you have worked on all spring in order to relax and maintain, a song that you cannot let go of because it makes you happy, or even looking at a special place that holds value, not in the sense of money, but the value of love and respect" (Travis Joy, Sacred Place–Sacred Space Class, 2010). Or it may be tangibly stored within physical matter present at a site, much like a song can be ingrained and stored on a vinyl record or CD—the physiological or psychological footprint of a person's life as they resided within, or journeyed through, a space. Individual or multiple activities that took place within a place at a time in history or over the course of history, can leave a minuscule trace, a tiny imprint, or a groove, in the wood, the stone, the land—the physical matter—of that space or place. This stored, or storied, memory can then connect with our mind and body in a variety of ways, or it may find a much deeper connection with our meta-physical existence—with the spirit of our mind or the soul of our body: "What is it about a place that awakens the sense that divinity breathes in this place more than elsewhere? Why is there a stillness in some places that allows the questions that set us aside from other animals to rise to the surface of our busy minds?" Perhaps in them, we find a "collective unconscious echo of memory" (Feehan, in *Abbey Leix Anthology*, Volume One, 2010, p. 78).

Another attribute of the physiological and psychology link with the sacred may relate to the physical placement of our human body within a place or space. Can the actual placement of our body assist in our ability to connect with the sacred?

Whether the result of nature's design, purposeful man-made design, mystical design, design through *storied memory* and the history of place, or the placement of our body within a place or space, mankind benefits in its search for the sacred by coming in physical contact with sacred places and sacred spaces. With everything from small glimpses, to grand visions, our contact with the sacred is meant to help us reconnect with life as it was intended to be. The more we experience such sites; the more we begin to research and understand their backgrounds, their original meanings, and their individual meanings for self; and the more we allow them to touch and activate our expanded imagination the more opportunities we have to discover and experience the sacred.

Chapter 7

Heywood Gardens, County Laois, Ireland

Chapter Eight
The Sacred and History

History is a product of change. Some say history is what it is; it does not change. But history is what we know of it at any given time. So history, in its most factual sense, does not change once it is set in place. But what it tells us, does change. It opens new messages and further details every day. It presents itself in innovative ways every year. And what it tells me, may be different than what it tells you. With something as simple as taking a trip, meeting a new person, or writing a note in a journal, we change history for the future. History for our children will be what we make of our lives and our environment today. History for us is what our parents and those who came before us, made it to be. If we uncover that history and apply it to our lives and our environment, we grow. If we leave it uncovered, it dies and we die.

The sacred is often hidden in history, in historical events, or at historical sites, all the way back to nature's nativity. The knowledge of this history helps determine a place or object's sacred significance.

The lives and actions of those who have passed before us leave their mark, their sign, for us to uncover so that we might connect. Ruins leave their history for us to unearth. Written words leave their story to be unfolded. Music leaves it sounds and its traditions to reverberate. Photos, drawings, and icons leave their symbols to decipher. It is all still there, present forever in the memory of the stones, the earth, the landscape, the walls, and the objects left behind. Some people have the unique ability to recognize, and identify with, this memory residing in matter—to connect with what happened, good or bad, through past emotions safely secured in a specific location, or in a specific material object. Others can learn to recognize this history through continued exposure, openness, and exploration. New inhabitants and new explorers have the capability to develop a relationship with a historic place through its documented history, its *storied memory*, and its past-presence—the mystery of presence that dwells within the sacred throughout time.

Chapter 8

Garden Door, Paris, France

Chapter Nine
The Sacred and the Senses

hile science calls for continual and repeated examination of our thoughts and images, sometimes the sacred beckons for sensory insight into our "first time" images and experiences. Time and again, this first image is the purest (Bachelard, 1994, p. 156).

Though my journey into the study of sacred place and sacred space began with a crow's enchanted dance on the Eastern Band of the Cherokee Indian Reservation, my senses were impassioned by the splendor of Ireland. It is an enchanting land of landscape and people. I have never felt more at home, and alive, than in Ireland.

As my wife and I flew into Dublin Airport, Ireland, eleven years ago, the first thing we experienced was bewilderment. Attempting to navigate our rental car through Dublin's roundabouts and rush hour traffic while driving on the other side of the road had us both tense and confused. Our first of countless friendly encounters in Ireland came from a lorry driver who saw our obvious distress and called from his open window, "Where you heading?" "Abbeyleix" we replied. "Right. Follow me." Off he went, and off we followed.

Out of the bustle of Dublin City we were soon in awe of the vivid greenness of the land and its puzzle pieces of earth divided by ancient stack stone walls. It was magical. We had never seen anything like this intensity of beauty.

Since that first excursion in Ireland, we now fly into Shannon, and take the back roads across the island. Most of these roads have improved since our first visit, especially with the new motorway, which makes for much faster and easier travels. But, to truly experience Ireland, the older routes and roadways are still the best.

Our trips have taken us to most every region of Ireland except Northern Ireland. We have trekked from Dublin to Shannon and many places in between. From the southernmost parts of Ireland to the Western Coast of Dingle. To Connemara in the Northwest, to the midlands of County Laois. We have visited over one hundred sacred sites in Ireland, including holy wells, grand cathedrals, the Burren, faeire rings, the Mass Rock of Oughaval, Glendalough, the Cliffs of Moher, the Slieve Bloom Mountains, the Rock of Dunamase, round towers and castles, ancient cemeteries with their Celtic High Crosses and historic portal tombs like Poulnabrone, woodlands and farmland full of Jackdaw ravens, tidy towns, villages, wilderness homes of saints and monks from days gone by, and countless expanses of magnificent forest land, bogs, and sublime landscapes.

Each of these sites offered something to touch the senses in its own unique ways. With some sites, I connected quickly; some took time and multiple visits; and there were other places with which I never quite connected. Yet, none failed in their offering of multisensory encounters with something beyond the ordinary. With some of

Chapter 9

these sites I came away with a bit of their mystery revealed. With most, I could sense the mystery and the sacred, but their essence remained intact, embedded forever in the fabric of matter, space, and time. A time and consistency created by man, nature, and God.

I have found that the greatest sensory encounters of the sacred occur when I am open to sensory stimulation, but not overtly seeking a particular sensation. Mystery and the sacred cannot be forced to reveal themselves. They require a communion of the senses, the sacred, and the spirit of mankind for this to take place. But for me, if ever there was a place where this sacred essence and mystery is closest to the surface, it is in Ireland. Here the land is alive and vibrant. Everything offers opportunity for sensory overload, but in a most constructive manner. The rain is wetter, the wind stronger, the cold colder, the air crisper, the colors more vivid, the sounds sharper, the textures thicker, smells more aromatic, tastes more flavorful, and thin spots thinner. Just below the façade of these physical sensory allurements lies a multi-sensory, meta-sensory experience waiting to be set free in the home place of our souls.

It is often through the stimulation of the physical senses that one first encounters the sacred. Sacred places and sacred spaces, by design, appeal to our senses. They trigger specific sensory-stimulatory detectors in our body, through the avenue of smells, tastes, sounds, visuals, textures, forms, feelings, and emotions, and then request a response.

We are each sensitive to the sacred in varying degrees, based on our past experiences. Positive past experiences create positive physio-psycho changes in our physical chemistry and negative experiences create negative physio-psycho changes in chemistry—each offering a sense-response or lack of response accordingly. These often-programmed reactions are strongly related to our upbringing, our lifestyle, and our educational training, an extended part of our past experiences. They are also actively related to our new experiences, our current emotional state of being, and our openness to both the known and the unknown. The sacred can touch our analytical mind as well as our imagination, our creativity, and our intuitive nature (O'Donohue, *Anam Cara*, 1998, pp. 84-88).

To gain new experiences and uncover the sacred, it is imperative that we visit documented sacred sites, but it is likewise important that we are open for extra-sensory stimulation to occur anywhere around us, even when not actively seeking out a sacred site. Sometimes the sacred is uncovered in the most unexpected places, and a new sacred place or space is born. This sacred site may only be sacred to us, but if more and more people become aware of it, it may become a documented sacred site and become knighted as such by a title.

Unlike the common notion of a sixth sense, I have come to believe that each of our five physical senses is a conduit to a higher level of sensory stimulation. We can see, feel, taste, smell, and hear with our mind and body, but we can also see, feel, taste, smell, and hear with our spirit and soul, thus opening an avenue to transcend the physical and reach beyond into the spiritual or the sacred. Sacred places and spaces enhance the opportunity and ability for this to occur. We begin to hear on a physical plane, but within a sacred place or space, we are more apt to move beyond the physical and encounter the sacred.

Each of our senses are meant to transport us into a deeper, richer, sacred realm, yet we often become content with physical experiences and simplistic emotions without giving thought to where they might lead. We think we have achieved the summit of the experience, so we stop the journey. We smile, we laugh, we shout, we cry, then we go back to our mundane existence without realizing how close we were to a true connection with the sacred.

Chapter 9

How do we uncover this sacred essence beneath the physical façade of what we simply see, feel, taste, smell, and hear? By learning to experience the senses with our spirit, and not simply our mind.

The Senses in Action—Experiential Learning

By viewing sacred landscapes we unearth holy vision; by hearing sacred sounds we experience the music of the spheres; by touching sacred items we feel and caress the sacrosanct; by smelling sacred scents we absorb the aroma of the hollowed; and by tasting the sacred we commune with the creation and our Creator in the life-sustaining ritual we call eating.

Sight

Upon encountering the sacred, people often refer to the place or space by using the visual term *beautiful*, or in their descriptive talk they speak of an intensity of beauty that was both seen and felt. Sight is often the first way we encounter a sacred place. We are initially inspired visually, and in our minds we create a mental expression of sacred significance. We are touched by imagery, shapes, forms, vast open spaces, or colors, and our emotions are heightened, more so then during normal occurrences. These visuals of the sacred paint a picture for us about a time, place, event, or story that has sacred significance, and we, through our seeing, gain vision into something more meaningful than outward expression can communicate. We might also experience and express the sense of sight metaphorically through our use of words: *I see how you feel that way or I see what you mean.*

Potential Sacred Sight Encounters

- Connecting with nature's beauty and power as seen in the ancient stonewall-sectioned Irish landscape, or the grand expanse of the Alaskan wilderness.
- Viewing the soft feminine beauty of the Tennessee Smoky Mountains, or the rough and masculine splendor of the Black Hills and Badlands of South Dakota.
- Observing the storm-fed fast-moving River Ganga in India, or the gentle flow of Cooper Creek in Bryson City, with fishing pole in hand.
- Witnessing the visual brilliance of a Florida Keys' sunset, or the Great Northern Lights—Aurora Borealis.
- Watching a flock of birds create geometric patterns in the sky, a lone deer grazing in a field, or a spider spinning her web.
- Examining and identifying the shapes and colors of stones, plants, soil, and cloud formations in the sky, or experiencing the complete darkness of a cave.
- Studying sacred symbols as illustrated in an ancient Irish manuscript, or viewing the stick figure drawings of a child.
- Being captivated by the multi-colored lights dancing through a stained-glass window, or the solitary flicker of a candle at night.
- Identifying the elaborate details in an English cathedral that are meant to create a visual gateway to the sacred, or slowly being stirred by the simplicity of wooden pews and open windows in a historic church in Cades Cove.
- Responding to the geometric and mathematical perfection of a grand historic church, or the geometric irregularity found in the sacred presence in nature.

Sound

Words and other natural sounds that are made by people, and nature (the reading of books, listening to music, hearing the noises made by plants, animals, insects, water, wind), all have living energy within them. Sounds are created by vibrations being made by something, or someone, and these vibrations are then perceived by sound receptors within someone or something else. We experience the world through these sound vibrations and make sense of it, or are confused by it, accordingly.

Words are perhaps my favorite sacred sounds. They are composed of symbols arranged into meaningful formats that create value for the hearer. I am a collector of words, and enjoy them in their written and illustrated form the most. Allowing them time to roll over and over within my mind and spirit as they seek my personal interpretation. In-spirit, I pronounce them with accents, intensity, and emphasis, until I am content with their worth. When accomplished in silence, this task is like a meditation. When done aloud, my wife would beg to differ. I hold them in as often as possible, but at times they rush forth, bringing my grandchildren to vocal merriment!

Music, whether provided by voices, instruments, or nature herself, works on and in people because we are not solid mass. "Our bodies are instead, great conventions of whirling atoms which somehow find kinship to form molecules, and which then clump together into tissue, bones, and blood. Throughout our bodies there is a great amount of empty space, which allows other environmental forces to move through us, as well as giving our ever-moving molecules the ability to form harmonic alignments" (Swan, 1990, p 139). All humans identify with sound and especially with diverse styles of music. As music is heard and felt, our bodies come in-tune and begin molecularly to play in response to the music. The sense of sound can also be experienced metaphorically through a variety of words and phrases: *I hear you or I can almost hear it*, referring more to an understanding of something or almost understanding a concept or idea.

Potential Sacred Sound Encounters

- Taking notice of the natural sounds of animals, insects, water, wind, or storms while walking in the woods, or the sounds of the cicadas while enjoying an English pipe on your back porch.
- Attentively listening to the succession of musical tones as presented by the various instruments played during a classical concert, or the four-part harmony of a church choir or group of Christians worshiping God.
- Concentrating on the melodious chanting of monks in an Irish monastery, or the wavering notes of sacred harp singers in a white-washed church in the Smoky Mountains.
- Listening to the fervent prayer of an inspiring spiritual leader, or praying a simple prayer in silence within your mind or spirit.
- Trying to heed the words of advice from a friend, or seeking out a quiet place to spend time in silence, alone with your thoughts.
- Repeating the words of sacred scripture again and again, or reading a good and relaxing novel to release the stresses of the day.

Touch

To comprehend touch, we must experience it. Through touch, we personally encounter the world, and in so doing, we have the opportunity to encounter the sacred. Through touch we can connect not only with the physical and symbolic representation of someone or something, but also with previously unidentifiable phenomena—the spiritual essence, or storied memory, of the person or object. We metaphorically touch God through our encounters with sacred places, and sacred items. Or, perhaps, we truly touch God.

Chapter 9

As humans, we are meant to touch and be touched. I believe the entire creation-kingdom experiences this need as well. Through the action of touch, we receive and release energy, we feel and share life. By *physically* touching someone, we can also touch them with our soul, and through words of love and encouragement spoken, we can touch someone with our spirit. It is perhaps the most intimate expression of love we can share (Hilliard, 2006).

Some studies have shown that our bodies are weakened by the wearing of synthetic fabric—this is not the case with natural fabrics. Synthetic materials carry a negative electrical field, possibly causing negative responses as natural-human and un-natural fields combine (Swan, 1990, pp 22 & 146). Could, therefore, a world consumed with synthesized materials dull the ability to connect, through touch, with the natural and the sacred? The sense of touch can also be experienced and expressed metaphorically: *I was touched by what you said, I was touched by your presence,* or *That was very touching.*

Potential Sacred Touch Encounters

- Touching our spouse with a passionate kiss or sexual encounter, or offering a holy, non-sexual, kiss to a friend.
- Lifting of holy hands to touch God in praise or worship, or holding the hand of a dying parent.
- Feeling the various textures, shapes, and forms provided in nature (a tree, a plant, water, or stone), or experiencing the man-made implements used in worship.
- Walking a battlefield full of history and pain, or walking barefoot in a mountain stream.
- Moving our body in dance, exercise, a hike, or a meditative pursuit, or physically moving our residence across the world to a new country.

- Touching opposites (cold/hot, rough/soft, small/large), or touching things that are similar, to understand common relationships.
- Touching, or otherwise coming in contact with, the four earth elements (fire, air, water, earth), or allowing ourselves to be touched (metaphorically or spiritually) by our world.
- Contacting the physical through the act of writing, painting, drawing, or sculpting, or experiencing the touch of God in our art, our daily activities, or in our sacred worship.
- Placing or touching the furnishings in a tabernacle or place of worship, or designing a private place or space for sacred activity (like a room in your home) through the placement of furnishings and symbols.
- Touching someone through our words or actions, or touching someone with our hands during a massage.

Smell

Smell is one of the strongest sensual engagers of memory. Various smells can take us back to a personal memory that occurred in the past, or smells can stimulate a connection to stored or *storied memory* that belonged to someone or something else—*storied memory* in a piece of antique furniture, in the walls of a house, or on the soil of a battlefield.

Smells can also represent the essence of their source (a plant or other item from which the smell originates). The sacred nature within, can be expressed without, through smell.

Smell is the sense most closely related to taste. Without smell, taste is greatly diminished. With the combining of smell and taste the essence of a plant or other food is intensified. Many of the smells we encounter can be captured or synthesized to offer the art and science of aromatherapy. With natural methods, the scent is extracted directly from a plant. In synthesized methods, artificial smells are created to mimic the true scent. The natural essence or smell is superior to the synthetic version for a potential sacred encounter.

The term *smell* can also be used metaphorically: *This just doesn't smell right*, when talking about something that does not appear to be true, safe, or beneficial.

Potential Sacred Smell Encounters

- Sensing the sacred smells of incense or candles burned in a worship service, or these same smells used during personal meditation or for medicinal purposes.
- Studying the ancient practice of making animal sacrifices that offered up pleasing aromas before God, or taking part in the ritual of sacrificing/offering non-animal products from nature like tobacco, oil, sage, cedar, or sweet grass.
- Making ourselves aware of the natural smells provided by plants, soil, rain, minerals, the ocean, and storms, or consciously acknowledging the smells we create when cooking spicy foods.
- Placing containers of smell-producing products around the home such as tobacco, cinnamon, fruit, sage, natural candles, or flowers instead of using synthesized products, or opening all the windows in the home to allow nature's smells to flow through the space.

Taste

Within the mouth are hundreds of taste receptors, yet we devour our food so quickly that we seldom experience the true flavors—their essence. To experience the flavors presented through the sense of taste, we must slow down and savor the textures, tastes, and smells of our food. This process of slow-eating allows us to activate multiple taste receptors and better experience the taste-essence of our food (Hilliard, 2006).

Sharing food and the gift of tasting food with others through a communal meal is a life-sustaining ritual and in and of itself has a sacred quality. Likewise, the individualized ritual of fasting has a sacred quality—a practice in which we do not eat for a given period of time in dedication to thought, worship, prayer, or meditation.

The term *taste* can also be used metaphorically: *He has very bad taste in friends*. Just like certain foods may taste bad to us, some actions or activities can be in bad taste.

Potential Sacred Taste Encounters

- Tasting natural foods and plants over a communal meal with family or friends, or a taking part in a communal meal of bread and wine with God and fellow worshipers.
- Slowly appreciating the individual and intense flavors of a meal cooked by a gourmet chef and attempting to identify each flavor, or eating a hotdog over a wilderness campfire with your family.
- Tasting fresh mountain water flowing downward from the snow covered Rocky Mountains, or enjoying a morning cup of Irish tea from the comfort of your home or back deck.
- Chewing food multiple times before swallowing while attentively contemplating each bite, or tasting and comparing four varieties of red wines.
- Enjoying the sense of taste through the eating of food, water, wine, oils, or grains that may be prepared and used in a sacred ritual, or taking pleasure in eating a piece of freshly picked fruit directly from its natural source.

Chapter 9

- Eating when you are hungry rather than eating at set times each day, or setting aside the gift-portion or spirit-portion of a meal by placing a small quantity of your meal on a plate and setting it outside to be devoured by nature as a gift.
- Spending time contemplating the concept of good taste (metaphorically) as it relates to you and the way you present yourself, or experiencing a different type of food each week or once per month (food items you are not familiar with), or promote your knowledge of foods by spending time researching the food, its source, its ingredients, and its health benefits.

Does Nature Sense Us

One of the questions presented by my study of sacred place and space and the senses, is whether places and spaces feel and experience us as we do them? Obviously, the environment is sensitive to the actions of mankind, but does it feel in the same way as we humans feel. Do places and spaces, and does nature experience the joy and pain and sadness as humans do? Does nature dream? I believe Saint Paul addresses this question well in his letter to the Christian church in Rome around A.D. 57, when he states that "since the creation of the world His [God's] invisible attributes, His eternal power and divine nature, have been clearly seen, being understood through what has been made ... For the anxious longing of the creation waits eagerly for the revealing of the sons of God. For the creation was subjected to futility, not willingly, but because of Him who subjected it, in hope that the creation itself also will be set free from its slavery to corruption into the freedom of the glory of the children of God. For we know that the whole creation groans and suffers the pains of childbirth together until now" (Romans 1:20 & 8:19-22, New American Standard Bible).

This Biblical text shares the concept of nature as a living, breathing, feeling entity. If accepted as a literal discourse on nature, it appears that all of creation, including mankind and nature (trees, plants, flowers, water, stone, landscape, wildlife, mountains, earth, and sky, and all the elements within the realms of earth and sky), experience the joys and pains that being a living creature produces. As we experience nature, it senses us back. As we encounter creation through sight, sound, touch, smell, and taste, nature sees us, hears us, touches us, smells us, and tastes us. It is a reciprocal and shared encounter of sensory inspiration and stimulation. This then begs the question, is the reciprocal action between the two forms of life one of encouragement or detriment? Man and nature are intended to join together in unity. Nature shares with mankind the invisible attributes of God. Nature, thus, presents the most active sacred elements known to this planet. Through nature and her elements, we encounter God. Through the use of the elements of nature, we build places to celebrate God, to encounter the sacred. I have come to believe that nature and her elements offer the greatest material passageway into the sacred. Through an appropriate relationship with nature and through an appropriate use of natural elements in the structuring of sacred places, we create places around which, and through which, the spiritual energy of the sacred can freely flow by means of the fabric we call space. Through the channel of space, that which is spiritual, threads its way through the creation. Sometimes our senses perceive this thread in an open space, sometimes in a specific place. Our physical senses are aroused, and we are transported to the beyond. We move beyond the metaphor.

We best learn to sense nature by understanding that she senses us back. How do we want to be perceived and remembered? Appropriate thoughts and environmentally sensitive actions result in greater sensory reception and understanding. They offer grander sacred encounters. If we, metaphorically or literally, sense something as bad for the earth or nature, it is likely bad for mankind as well. And, if we sense something as bad for mankind, it is likely bad for nature. *Oh, what does the earth dream, as our garden slumbers? Of the same things that we dream*—renewal, wholeness, well-being, gratitude, and love.

Chapter 9

In addition to nature, God's Holy Word, as provided in ancient Biblical scripture, is also a part of His creation. As such, it supplies the creation (mankind and nature) answers to the many questions we pose toward a sustainable and enjoyable existence. Human creations—art, music, and the written and illustrated word, can likewise offer inlets for people and nature to sense a meaningful presence, connection, and purpose in and with the world. As an artist moves into the meta-physical realm of actuality, he rises above symbols as metaphors and enters a world of creative ethereality

Family Burial Ground, Smoky Mountains National Park

Chapter Ten
The Sacred and Ritual: Spirit-Ritual

During the summer of 2004, I introduced a group of college students to the Eastern Band of the Cherokee Indian Reservation for a one-week short course I taught, entitled *Exploring Spirituality in Sacred Place and Sacred Space*. The course consisted of morning and evening discussions about these phenomena, with the afternoons devoted to experiential learning in nature or at Cherokee sacred sites, including taking part in a multiplicity of cultural rituals. Two of the most memorable rituals were a Cherokee Sweat Lodge Ceremony and a traditional Sacred Pipe Ritual. I had arranged for a local Cherokee/Lakota Medicine Man to allow myself and my class to take part in a sweat ceremony he conducts each Wednesday evening.

We arrived at the ceremonial ground mid-afternoon and began to collect twenty-four "grandfather" stones, each a bit larger than softballs. We than assisted the Medicine Man in laying a two-foot-tall fire-pit of wood, atop which the stones were placed. The fire was lit and burned intensely until just before dark—approximately 3 hours.

The ceremonial sweat lodge was already erected, created by arching willow and other pliable branches into the ground, upward, over, and down into the ground about ten feet across, creating a ten-foot diameter dome-hut about six feet in height at its center. Atop the hut were fitted large tanned animal skins of buffalo and deer, each hide overlapping the others to form a tight seal. One out of place quilted blanket lay off to the right top of the dome. A flap of hide was left loose at the front of the lodge, to be used as an entrance and exit. Inside at the center, was a stone fire pit into which the Medicine Man placed the twenty-four hot and glowing grandfather stones. A large container of water was also placed inside the lodge, near the entrance. Not for drinking, but to pour over the stones during the ceremony.

Just before dusk, we were joined by eighteen very large, very naked Native American men, some Cherokee, some Lakota, and a Cherokee Elder and Medicine Man from Georgia, who had been invited to oversee the evening's sweat.

I had assumed we would participate in a mild "tourist sweat." I was wrong. As we entered the lodge, I found out that this evening's ceremony was to be special. Not because we were the honored non-native guests, but because the Cherokee Tribal Council was in session the following day to debate and vote whether to allow the Lakota Sun Dance Ceremony to be introduced to the tribe and officially approved as an Eastern Band Cherokee Reservation ritual. While the local Lakota wished to introduce this ritual, the local Cherokee disapproved because it is not a traditional Cherokee ceremony. On this night, these eighteen tribal members were present to conduct this pre-ceremonial sweat lodge ritual to guide the next day's decisions.

To begin the evening's ceremony, my group lined up behind the Indian participants. We then walked counterclockwise around the lodge three times, several Cherokee and Lakota chanting as we moved. We entered the lodge through the open flap, one at a time, with our Indian hosts sitting in the outer circle of the interior space and my group of eight sitting on the inner-circle around the fire-pit of radiant, glowing stones. Water was poured on the stones, and the door-flap was closed. Utter darkness—except for the burning hot red stones.

What I remember most from the next half hour is the concentrated intensity of the heat. Each breath was beyond painful, as if wet, hot, liquid coals were being forced into the mouth and down into the lungs. Sweat was pouring from my body, and my temples began to contract and pound, as my mind began to drift into nowhere, or perhaps into everywhere. I have never experienced such a state of dazed intoxication as at that very minute. The feeling of being drugged, mixed with the pounding of my head, was not pleasant. I wanted out!

The sounds around me included everything from laughter, to chanting, to praying, to crying—all in a tomb of complete darkness. Some spoke in the Cherokee language, some in Lakota, some in English. It was another world. About thirty minutes into the ritual, the Medicine Man overseeing the ceremony opened the flap, and cool air swept into the lodge with welcoming appreciation. The Elder began to share words about the next day's council gathering and address some of the men's chants. Though participants are not to leave the lodge until the ceremony is complete—after four openings of the door-flap—this was the time to exit, should anyone feel it necessary. One Cherokee, one Lakota, left. Water was added to the stones, filling the lodge with a blanket of steam and a loud *hiss*. The flap was once again closed.

About fifteen minutes later, the flap was re-opened, and more words of wisdom were offered by our leader as he literally held back one of my students and three Indians from exiting by blocking the passageway with one of his arms. At the end of his words, he lowered his hand. My student exited, the three Indians, and myself. I wish to state that my reason for leaving was to comfort my student, which was indeed true, but I also wished to comfort myself. As we sat on a wooden bench outside the lodge, I placed my arm around the student as she cried, emotions tumbling unrestrained from her shaking body. After several minutes, we quietly talked about her emotions as she spoke of her father. Even now as I write this, it brings storied-tears to my eyes.

Two more times the flap opened, the Medicine Man spoke, with a few more participants exiting each round. At the end of the ceremony, only eight remained. Four were my students. For these four, almost two hours had passed since they entered the lodge. Two hours of intense heat and extreme emotional and physical strain, but they each were taking home the memory of a lifetime. That evening, when back at the comfort of our air-conditioned cabin, we each discussed our experiences while taking part in the ceremony. I was impressed by everyone's reflections, but I was especially struck by the reasons the four students stayed to the bitter-end. Their motivations ranged from pure physical will power to overcome an obstacle, to an inner desire to gain a spiritual lesson or personal enlightenment from their encounter.

My personal reflection? I was very grateful I had the opportunity to participate in this amazing ceremony. I had gained new insights never to be forgotten and made new Cherokee and Lakota friends in the process. And I will never do a sweat lodge ceremony again! We each find our sacred place and sacred space at times when we need them. Some places connect with some individuals, some with others. This was not my sacred place, but I have been blessed to experience many other places and spaces that are.

Rituals have a multiplicity of purpose: they assist the participant in engaging in a process; they cleanse and prepare the individual

Chapter 10

for something to happen; they connect people, places, history, and traditions; and they affect the place at which the rituals occur. But they can also obstruct our connection with the sacred if they lose their essential purpose.

Ritual, in its purest sense, is a spiritual activity and should lead us to that which is sacred. Yet, in its most conventional form, ritual has become nothing more than a rote formula to be followed with precision and care. Our ritual—our habit—has become one in which we follow ritualistic activity, as a physical endeavor only. It has become mundane and routine (Hilliard, 2006). "Sometimes our spiritual programmes take us far away from our inner belonging. We become addicted to the methods and programmes of psychology and religion" (O'Donohue, *Anam Cara*, 1998).

So how do we return to ritual as a spiritual, or sacred, activity? We begin by exploring the spiritual thread that weaves its way through all that is sacred. True spirituality is *spirit-ritual*, or doing what we do—ritual—with our spirits and our souls and not just our minds and our bodies. The biggest obstacle in our ability to encounter the sacred, is that our ritual has lost its spirit. With our most common methodologies for worshiping God or taking part in spiritual activity, or essentially in any daily ritual, we walk through the steps, but we do not engage our spirit. We must learn, or relearn, to involve our individual spirits in our spiritual activity and our daily activity. Our ritual must become spirit-ritual, if our intent is to connect with that which is sacred. It is a connection we can only make in-spirit, in sacred space.

Historically recorded accounts of sacred transcendence into spiritual realms have resulted from rituals, at sacred places, or in isolation in the nature (Swan, 1990).

We tend to have the misunderstanding that our spirits and our souls are entities that we will only use when we are physically dead and no longer reside on this earth. This belief is far from the truth and restrains and confines our capability to encounter the sacred during our typical seventy to one-hundred years of physical existence. Our spirits and souls are not meant to be held in reserve while we walk this earth. Their intended purpose is to be every bit as active as their physical counterparts— our minds and bodies.

The Spirt, Soul, Mind, and Body

If we are to activate our spirits and our souls while living our human lives, what precisely are they, and how do we stimulate them into action? We have a physical mind that resides within our physical body. This mind is the thinking, feeling, cognitive, rational, and emotional part of our body. When stimulated, the body responds accordingly. Likewise, we have a spiritual mind—the spirit—the counterpart to our physical mind. This spirit is the thinking, feeling, meta-cognitive, super-rational, and meta-emotional part of our soul. Our soul is the meta-physical counterpart of the physical body, just as the spirit is the meta-physical counterpart of the mind. So, we have a physical mind, and a spiritual mind—the spirit. We have a physical body, and a spiritual body—the soul. The spirit is stimulated, and the soul responds.

"For who among men knows the thoughts of a man except the spirit of the man which is in him" (I Corinthians 2:11, New American Standard Bible) and "My spirit has rejoiced in God my Savior" (Luke 1:47, New American Standard Bible). Similar Biblical analogies are given for the soul and body: "The Lord makes me lie down in green pastures; He leads me beside quiet waters, He restores my soul" (Psalm 23: 2-3, New American Standard Bible) and "As the deer pants [thirsts] for water, so my soul pants [thirsts] for God (Psalm 42: 9, New American Standard Bible). In these scriptures, we are helped to understand the spirit via parallels with the mind— knowledge and emotion; and the soul via parallels with the body— the physical need for rest and nourishment [water]. I do not believe these comparisons are coincidence, nor simple metaphors. God is helping us understand the spirit and the soul via their physical counterparts the mind and our body. The spirit and soul of the human being are every bit as real as the human mind and body, and every bit as capable of engagement and interaction.

In addition, within the physical mind lies the physical conscience—the part of our mind that motivates us to do things out of fear or other self-directed benefits (we obey the law to avoid getting caught and punished, we are faithful to our spouse because she might divorce us, etc.). The spiritual counterpart to our conscience is the heart—our meta-conscience. The heart abides within the spirit, just as the conscience lives within the mind. With our heart, we are inclined to do things because they are the right things to do. "Your words have I treasured in my heart, that I may not sin against you" (Psalm 119:11, New American Standard Bible). "They [the Gentiles] show the work of the Law written in their hearts, their conscience bearing witness and their thoughts alternately accusing or else defending them" (Romans 2:15, New American Standard Bible).

While living on this earth, our spirits and our souls reside within our minds and bodies and are often totally confined by such because of our self-limiting understanding of the spiritual aspect of life. Spirit-Ritual provides an avenue by which our spirits and souls, while residing within our physical bodies, can be lifted to a higher plane of existence. Spirit-Ritual provides a way for our spirits and souls to move beyond our self-imposed restraints and connect our minds and bodies with the sacred. Our spirits then use our minds, and our souls use our bodies, to accomplish physical activity (both big and small), on a spiritual level, or as sacred activity. Contact with that which is sacred is the catalyst for this meta-physical/spiritual action to occur. "The spirit conceives neither seasons, nor distances, nor any other limiting definitions" (Ruth Beebe Hill, 1979, p. 105—Writer, Professor of Lakota Culture).

This does not imply that the spirit, the soul, and the heart cannot be lead into darkness and despair, but that they, as the spiritual counterparts of our physical entities, must be activated by a sacred source, the Spirit of God, to avoid such occurrence. "The Spirit of Truth, whom the world cannot receive, because it does not see Him or know Him, but you know Him because He abides with you and will be in you" (John 14: 17, New American Standard Bible). "You are not in the flesh, but in the Spirit, if indeed the Spirit of God dwells in you. But, if anyone does not have the Spirit of Christ, he does not belong to Him. If Christ is in you, though the body is dead because of sin, yet the spirit is alive because of righteousness. But if the Spirit of Him who raised Jesus from the dead dwells in you, He who raised Christ Jesus from the dead will also give life to your mortal bodies through His Spirit who dwells in you" (Romans 8:9-11, New American Standard Bible).

In actuality, all humans are spiritual and experience and express spirituality, even if unaware, because we each possess a spirit and a soul. But much too often our spirituality is limited by unbelief, by trying to accomplish things only on a physical level, or by trying to accomplish things guided by our human spirits apart from the Creator of our spirits. In doing so, we are *one Spirit short* in becoming a true spiritual being and in accomplishing true spiritual activity, in experiencing true religion, and in being able to connect with the essence of the sacred within a sacred place or space.

My conclusion—to encounter sacred place and space, we must do so through spirit-ritual. We must do so *in-spirit*—in and with our human spirit. If it is to be an all-encompassing sacred encounter, we must do so *In-Spirit*—in and with God's Spirit. Our spirits, souls, minds, and bodies must encounter their Creator on their journey into sacred place or space to receive the ultimate benefits awaiting those who enter. The Spirit of God becomes the Supreme Spirit-Guide through all sacred place and space.

Heritage Park, Spring Hill, Tennessee

Chapter Eleven
The Sacred and Nature

Henry David Thoreau was a prolific writer about his experiences in nature, and one of the unique aspects of his journals was his focus on his local surroundings, the world of nature within his everyday reach and experience. For most who habitually journal, the subject matter is self. Thoreau "focuses explicitly on the world rather than his own soul. He observes the objects which make up the landscape rather than the conflicts that produce the self. Thoreau writes more about the ordinary creatures and plants around him than he does ordinary details of his life. He writes more about what happens on the rivers and hilltops around town than what happens on main street" (Young, 2009, p. 43). Why?

In Dr. James Swan's lifetime study of Eskimo, Native American, and Polynesian people and their sacred places, he concluded that nature has always offered some of the most powerful stimulation for sacred encounters and spiritual experiences. "Contact with nature's primal vitality stir deep waters inside us" (Swan, 1990, p. 81).

Man, being composed of nature's elements, cannot exist without a connection with nature (Casey, 1993, 2009).

In Search of Saint Colman Mac Duagh

On several of my research trips to Ireland, my students and I were blessed to be accompanied by Dr. John Feehan, our travel professor and sacred site guide. Dr. Feehan is a Professor of Agriculture at University College Dublin, and an expert on sacred places and spaces. Feehan's home is the Midlands of Ireland, where he has a very deeply rooted sense of place and knowledge. On one of our adventures, we went in search of where Saint Colman Mac Duagh lived as a hermit in 595 A.D. Our destination was a cave located in the forest land of the Burren, County Claire, Ireland. Saint Mac Duagh was educated as a monk at Saint Enda's Monastery in Inishmore, but soon thereafter sought sacred solitude for an extensive portion of his life, both in Inishmore and then in the Burren. This day we were headed to the Burren in search of Colman Mac Duagh.

We entered the Burren National Park afoot, by way of a landscape of eroded, moon-cratered limestone that appeared to extend for miles beyond my vision. My grandfather's words for a landscape such as this were, "You can see as far as you can see." If I had been blindfolded and dropped off in the middle of this land, I might think I was on the moon, except for the patches of green and brown grasses and purple and yellow flowers scattered among the cratered stone that marked the terrain. It was late May or early June, the sunniest season for the Midlands, and what flowers I saw were in bloom. Though I do not know their name, I do remember their vivid colors, hues that looked out of place, growing seemingly out of gray solid stone. We walked for a long while in this rugged landscape, and in addition to the plant life, I also remember corral and sea shell fossils embedded within the stone. Signs that spoke of a past land that once dwelled beneath water. During our entire walk, I remember wondering what drew Saint Mac Duagh to this coarse and primitive land. Surely he came by a different path than we, or at a time when

Chapter 11

this land was much more richly forested, or he would have turned back to Inishmore. The landscape of the formidable Burren has its unique charm, but to the sensory eye, it presents itself as vastly uninhabitable. Yet, inhabit this land Mac Duagh did, for over seven years.

We eventually reached our intended destination, the sacred dwelling place of Colman Mac Duagh, and the gray stone turned to lush green and woodland, a place where the bare stone left off and the forest began. Not an extensive forest, as I had somehow expected from legend and myth, but a land that was said to have once been dense with oaks, pines, and ash. Here, at the edge of the vast expanse of space we had walked, was the vestige of the land's history. A place where animal life could be heard and seen. The air seemed different, fresher, cooler—you could smell the wet earth—and small signs of long-ago human existence offered glimpses into their past. Perhaps we captured a momentary visual display, and a brief taste, of what Mac Duagh encountered when he first approached his Burren home over 1400 years ago.

There was an intense emotional awareness that we were standing where Mac Duagh once stood; walking where he walked; breathing the molecules of air that created the smells akin to those he had breathed; and I even said a prayer, where he likely prayed. We individually took a moment to enter the grotto-like cave he called his home, and each sat for a few brief moments in silence, contemplating the life this hermit monk lived during a time long-passed. I was trying not to romanticize what was most certainly a hard life, while likewise envisioning the enchantment of a life of solitude with nature. Nothing much remained at the site, except the small cave, the ruins of a stone oratory said to have been built by Mac Duagh, and a holy well—which during his time would have simply been the place where he drew his water to drink, where it bubbled from the ground; the place where he occasionally bathed; and the place where perhaps he mediated with God within the core of His creation. We were at a place where religion, nature, legend, and history joined hands. A place mixed with fabled lore and actual deed. A place filled with a storied past that had something to share. A place with a sacred history, within this wonder-land of nature.

Legend has it that Mac Duagh openly communicated with the animal life surrounding him as he read, prayed, meditated, and pondered life. As daily companions, he was said to have kept a pet rooster who awakened him in the morning, a pet mouse who awakened him for prayer in the night, and a pet fly who marked the page of any book he was reading, when he needed to take a break from his text. There is a similar legend about Saint Mochua of Timahoe in County Laois where a visual monument stands to tell the story. From my experience and study of cultural myths tied to actual people, legends like these are traditionally based on a foundation of fact, generously supplemented with enchanted details by those who impart history via the written, spoken, or illustrated word. But the moral of most any myth or legend, blended with fact, can be found in the *whole of the story* it has to tell, even if portions of that story are not to be interpreted as literal reality. A traditional view of the concept of myth is that these accounts are sacred stories utilizing a sensory language created to touch the soul and activate memory.

So, what was the storied history that Mac Duagh left for my group to unearth at this ancient sacred site in nature, and through our guide's shared mythical tales of Mac Duagh's way of life. And how does the sacredness of other similar sites, and their stories, help us understand what these places and spaces have to share, if we can but learn to listen to, and experience their individual narratives?

Lessons Learned from Mac Duagh: His Story and our Encounter with Nature

- When a bit of fancy is added to a story of old, it is usually laid as a blanket atop a life of hardship. We tend to romanticize about days and people of old—the good old days. While there is a bit of charm and a sense of enchantment in a life like Mac Duagh lived, we must also acknowledge the harsh reality of his daily life of difficulties just to stay alive, warm, fed, and well. These difficulties and hardships as well as times of good can be uncovered in a mythical tale, in the factual accounts of life and place, and within the actual land, landscape, relics, ruins, and other historical objects in and around the places people lived.

- Mac Duagh's dwelling place was not what I expected—it was more simplistic, raw. We have been trained to look for the sacred in the grandeur and the stately, but sacred sites are not always what we expect them to be, or where we expect them to be—sometimes they can be in a cave in the woods. While some sacred sites are well kept, others have been left for nature to regain her rightful place. Some sacred sites are very ornate, but that grandeur may be inappropriately adorned by mankind's inappropriate sense of the sacred, and may no longer offer valid meaning. Other sites, may be very simplistic in nature, as they should be. One thing for sure, if we think we know what we are looking for in a sacred site, we will likely miss it.

- Sometimes we must travel rough terrain (in reality or metaphorically) in order to reach a sacred place or space. Our personal journey to any sacred site must be contemplated before, during, and after, to gain full meaning from its story.

- Sacred sites in nature are often places where men and women like Mac Duagh withdrew from normal life—life regulated, understood, and restricted by its benefits to an ordinary existence—to a life without these traditional benefits in order to connect with God, self, and nature. In our journey toward the sacred, mankind will sometimes seek out places of silence to replace lives of constant sound, places of little to replace lives of much, places of peace to replace lives of chaos. We are looking to create a new story, a new song, and not to live the lyrics of another.

Today there seems to be a new "awareness of nature as revelation in the theological sense: even to the extent of being able to speak again of the earth as sacrament. In this context, we can look at the holy wells (such as found at Mac Duagh's cave) with new eyes, and try to touch what was there in the beginning: that balance of landscape and water which the antennae of the most spiritually attuned members of the first community responded to as peculiarly focused in the ineffable and mysterious relationship between man and the earth which is his home and yet seems to draw him to something greater above and behind." Our senses are programed to draw us to places where nature has not been smothered by human control, overlay, and destruction. There we find our own nativity (Feehan, *The Sacredness of Place* article, p. 5).

Nature as a Part of Sacred Creation

Nature has an order of her own at the hand of her Creator. Man coming from this Creator and from the dust of earth has the aptitude to connect with this order by spending time in the wild. Therein, the divine presence of God can be detected, away from manmade objects, more so than within the world of human creations. Something about the absence of familiar things, as we spend time in nature, allows our creative energy to connect with our Maker. There, in the woods, in the artistic content of nature, we encounter the sacred, we encounter God.

Dr. Roger Walsh, professor of Psychiatry, Philosophy, and Anthropology (1990, pp. 2-3), shares that the sacred in nature allows all humanity to become "creative artists." "Life can be ecstatic. There are experiences so profound and meaningful that life and the world seem nothing less than sacred. There are moments of such bliss that they outshine ordinary pleasures, moments of such love and compassion that we fall helplessly in love with all of creation. We see that we are the creation of the sacred, intimately and eternally linked to the sacred, and forever graced and embraced by the sacred."

Mystery and enchantment gently unfold from the shadows, just as the sun begins to rise as day awakens, and again as it begins to fade at the close of each day. In the softness of twilight, the nightscape begins to take form, offering its gentle embrace of goodbye to the day. Then, once again the earth and sky arise to greet each other at the touch of dawn's light. This magic repeats itself in the passing of the seasons. From spring to summer, from summer to fall, from fall to winter, then once again the homecoming of spring. The eternal flow of the seasons rolls ever forward since their creation by God, and man finds his place in each.

Connoisseurs of the sacred enchantment in nature find that rhythmic patterns like the ebb and flow of light and the ever-changing seasons provide sweet and comforting reminders of both God and nature's gifts to the human spirit, soul, mind, and body. In nature, we find a sacred home. She is not only beneath us and surrounding us, but she is within us as we are her.

Heywood Gardens, County Laois, Ireland

Chapter Twelve
Qualities of Sacred Encounters

Dr. James Swan notes multiple qualities and emotions that occur when people encounter the sacred:

- feeling drawn to a place or space;
- emotional arousal as one nears a specific place or space;
- transition from typical consciousness to a deeper or higher level of connectivity;
- a connection with authenticity—that which is real and true;
- the occurrence of unusual, non-typical events;
- a loss of being controlled by time and space;
- a feeling of unity—an identification with something (maybe an animal, a stone, a person, a tree, a building, a place in nature, etc.);

- a unity of opposites such as cold/hot or fear/peace;
- a feeling of joy or bliss; a feeling that there is a divine presence;
- the inability to express feelings or emotions appropriately; and
- a return to the norm with a renewed sense of purpose, peace, meaning, and/or love for nature and others (Swan, 1990, pp. 77, 104).

Margaret Laski (1961), an English journalist, novelist, literary biographer, and one of the greatest contributors of words and quotes to the *Oxford English Dictionary*, was drawn to study spirituality and religion even though she professed to be an atheist. One of her major contributions to religious studies can be found in her book, *Ecstasy*, where she examined accounts of religious and sacred experiences, which she preferred to call ecstatic experiences. In her research, Laski conducted interviews and reviewed a substantial number of textual reports of mystical and *ecstatic experiences*. Within these encounters, she found there were two major aspects of each experience: intensity and withdrawal. The length of each person's individual experience within the intensity phase was generally brief, sometimes up to an hour, but this was not the norm. If the intensity level remained beyond an hour, Laski labeled this extended phase as *afterglow*.

In expressing personal ecstatic encounters, people noted

- Experiences were accompanied by, or triggered by, physical sensations. These sensations were usually pleasurable—joy, purification, renewal, new knowledge, problem solving ability—with many sensations attributed to encountering God.
- Encounters were most often regarded as beautiful and beneficial.
- During the phase of intensity there was an emotional feeling of upward movement.

Chapter 12

- During withdrawal, there was a feeling of downward movement.
- Childhood was one of the most common times of ecstatic experience.
- Sexual love was one of the most common adult experiences of ecstasy.

Dr. Bachelard (1994) states that the sacred first excites us, then it asks us to participate. If we fail to participate, we only encounter a physical sensory emotion. If we choose to participate, we encounter the sacred.

When I visited Stonehenge and Salisbury in England, I took several hours examining these ancient standing stones from every angle possible. I have found that sacred experiences not only allow us to see things from a different angle and unique perspective, but by *physically* viewing things from different angles and perspectives, we can sometimes encounter the sacred as well—viewing a site from atop a hill or from a plane, car, or train; lying flat on the ground; closing one or both eyes; or focusing the attention through a camera or telescope. I wanted to interpret these stones with this big-picture view in mind. To see where the earth, the rising stone, and the sky all met. To envision the stones within their environmental context of present time and past. I followed my visits by researching the textual history of both sites to add to my experiential, visual perspective.

Stonehenge has gone through massive alterations since its beginning over 5000 years ago. Historically it has always been a place that inspired and offered a sense of mystery that is most often defined as sacred. It is a place of great archaeological, meta-physical history whose purpose appears to be in offering a physio-spiritual connection between the earth and the sky, the physical and the heavenly, and on a more practical level, in the marking of time. The site was probably originally built as a temple made of standing timber pillars, which were replaced by the standing stones about 2500 years later. The mystery remains as to who did the building and to whom the structure was built to worship—if indeed it was originally a place of worship. But no one seems to question some type of mystical, sacred significance attached to the site (Richards, *Stonehenge*, 2005).

Visits to sacred sites like Stonehenge undeniably offer the opportunity to experience many of the qualities of sacred encounters noted by Laska (1961), Swan (1990), and Bachelard (1994).

The question I always ask myself as a Christian when visiting ancient sites like Stonehenge and Salisbury in England, and numerous ancient sites in Ireland and around the world that seem to have at least some history of pagan activity, is that if the formation of these ancient sites was not originally created to glorify God or to connect with the creation, why do they feel sacred, and why do so many people—Christian and non-Christian—flock to them every year?

Facts uncovered in my research with Dr. Feehan as we visited dozens of sacred sites in Ireland, are that most, if not all, of these sacred sites are entwined with nature and our sense of creation. Though a tremendous number of them were pagan sites at one time, that period was often preceded or followed by times of Christian activity. Believers in God as the Creator often converted former pagan sites into places for Christian worship, creating a sacred, storied, overlap in history with which people who believe in God can still connect on a sacred level. Since nature began with God, God can never totally be removed from her presence. Throughout time, mankind can continue to find God, even in the most unlikely of places.

Rachael's Labyrinth, Buckhorn Inn, Gatlinburg, Tennessee

Chapter Thirteen
What is Place

hile the words *place* and *space* are often used interchangeably, in this study I will identify them by their differing qualities.

Place and Examples of Place

- A specific point in a space – a cemetery on a hillside or the location of a pile of stones in a field.
- A building or area used for a purpose – a house, a church building, an office, or a cabin in the woods.
- A portion of a space – a specific area of plants within a garden, the location of a desk in a room.
- A smaller area within a larger area – the center of a labyrinth, or a room within a house (though a room might also be considered a space inside a place).

- Somewhere you go – a destination like the mountains, the sea.
- A particular spot – the site of a tree, a mountain, a river, a holy well.
- A specific location – a town or city.
- A setting often defined by one or more of the five senses – a tangible, visible, or auditory setting such as a waterfall on a hillside which may be located purely by its sound, or a campfire located by its smell.

Important Aspects of Place

- The human body creates stronger bonds with place than with space. The body is always in a place in space. The body is limited by, or offered freedom by, other places that reside in the space that surrounds and flows through it.
- Place is not bordered by nothingness, it is a geometric expanse of space.
- Place is not simply an annex of space, but an integral component.
- We often define who we are by our sense of place, where we are from. If we lose our place, we lose a bit of our identity.
- Placelessness creates anxiety, depression, desolation, and illness.
- A historic example of our tie to place, is the use of banishment as a punishment.
- We tend to describe a place by its sensory expressions – colors, shapes, textures, materials, smells, and sounds.
- A place has an atmosphere and a personality that can change our mood instantly (physically, chemically, and emotionally).
- A place can invite us in, turn us away, or remain quiet or neutral.

Chapter 13

- Place has the power to direct our movements.
- One place differs in function from another place.
- As society has become more mobile, our connection to a specific place has changed. For some it has become more important, while for others, it has become less important. With this mobility, perhaps we are losing our sense of place.
- A place can provide shelter from the world or a place to commune with others.
- A place depends on the telling of its story to have meaning.
- A story depends on place, because every story *takes place* in a place.
- A place can be destroyed by fire, flood, earthquake, or humans.
- A place has intellectual form.

Cades Cove, Smoky Mountains National Park

Chapter Fourteen
What is Space

Space and Examples of Space

- A continuous expanse - a body of water, the sky, or the atmosphere in general.
- An open area - an undeveloped field or sweeping landscape.
- An area of land or open spot within an area of land that is typically without buildings - an island or a parking lot/space.
- An empty area between reference points - the time between day and night, or an open road between point A and B.
- The physical universe within/outside the earth's atmosphere.
- An unoccupied area - wilderness or the space between earth and the moon.
- All that is around us - the expanse in which all matter exists.

- That which is in-between, or inside of, matter – open passageways or gaps between the atoms that make up various objects (spaces in wood, in stone, inside our bodies).
- Something you go through, usually to get somewhere else – a hallway, a lawn, or a passageway.
- That which surrounds a place – the open space outside a building or an object.
- The area between the tangible five senses – the gap between hearing and seeing or between smelling and tasting.
- An interval – the quiet span between two musical notes.

Important Aspects of Space

- We must go through space to get to a place.
- While place is a geometrical institution, space is undefined by such form.
- We often use the dimensions of height, width, length to define a place – the space is what is in between these dimensions, but not necessarily limited by the dimensions.
- Space is not identified by solid matter, but rather by the regions between or outside the atoms that compose matter.
- Place relies on space – place cannot exist without space.
- Space is more difficult to identify and quantify than place.
- Space is more mysterious and less explainable than place.
- Space is not limited by walls or physical barriers.
- Space is nowhere and everywhere at the same time.
- We can never fully understand the space of space – it is an inexhaustible poetic theme.

Chapter 14

- While all places are not directly connected, perhaps all spaces are.
- While a place has intellectual form, a space has intellectual essence.

St. Michael and All Angels Church, Abbeyleix, Ireland

Chapter Fifteen
What Is Sacred Place

In her article "Jerusalem & Pilgrimages" Sara Jane Boss, Lecturer in Christian Theology, University of Wales, states that referring to something or someplace as sacred implies that God is present within or reveals Himself through or to His world and its people, places, times, and things (North and North, 2007).

A sacred place is a building, a piece of land, or a place within a larger space that presents the divine to mankind and renders God's glory to be activated in human life-activities; a place that offers a connection with the spiritual essence of all that is created (including the spirit and soul of man and the spiritual essence of nature and creativity); a place that draws us into it by touching our physical senses yet leads us beyond the physical into a level of spiritual or meta-physical encounterment; a place that offers a sense of unexplained peace and awe; a place that offers us security and safety from the world and what the world deems important; and/or a place where sacred memory is stored to be shared with those who are open to expose and experience it. It is a place often dedicated to sacred ritual (spirit-ritual) for higher purpose. A place in which meta-vision and knowledge are perceived as the spirit is awakened and a place where the spirit and soul are encouraged to come out and play. It is a place in which we encounter the sacred in contrast to the mundane. It can be said that God's presence is in all places, and I would agree, but perhaps God chooses to show His presence in some places more so than others, based on the activity occurring at a given place at a given time.

Dr. John Feehan notes that these sacred places are where we seek out additional meaning for life, much more so than we can find in the common practices of our daily lives. "The essence our human spirit breathes at such places is the most fundamental ingredient in the intrinsic sacredness of place. And although you occasionally feel its touch in poetry, or in a painting, or as softly as the touch of a feather on your cheek, there is no substitute for the experience, for only in the woods or by the stream can it reach into and touch you" (Feehan, in *Abbey Leix Anthology*, Volume One, 2010, p. 79).

What makes a place sacred is the connection and communication it helps create between man and God, man and his spirit, man and the world in which he lives, man and nature. A place can become sacred if any of these entities are present. We consecrate it with the presence of our spirit and soul, with the spirit-essence in nature, or as we invoke the presence of God in a place through spirit-ritual—worship, prayer, song, meditation, purposeful intent—inviting God in for communion. Without the presence of spirit, soul, or spiritual essence, there is no sacred in place.

The often audibly inexpressible story of a place must find a way to communicate with those whose seek its story. One way this happens is through ontological amplification whereby the nature of our existence is aroused by being in a special place in which God's presence is animatedly alive—a sacred place.

Chapter 15

People and Sacred Place

A thorough description of a sacred place must include the people who live, work, play, worship, and make life decisions within a place. We gather in places to participate in life, and the decisions we make in these places can affect the well-being of all who take part. These decisions can affect one, the few, or the many. And these gathering places themselves have the ability to influence the decisions and the outcomes of the decisions made within them.

Purpose for Sacred Place

Places differ in their contributions to society, thereby granted the ability to become sacred based on their contributions (Casey, 1993, 2009).

A sacred place is meant to preserve and nurture the spirit and soul, and in so doing it nourishes the human mind and body as well. A sacred place guards us from physical and spiritual discord, it protects us from the arrows of hate and anger, self-centeredness, and pride—the abuses that being human in a physical world lay upon us every day.

Much too often our sacred places have become nothing more than tourist destinations, with more regard for entertainment within, than enlightenment. Massive flocks of tourists to sacred places have a significant effect on the potential intimacy such places have to offer. Large crowds and excessive noise can overshadow the sacredness of an otherwise sacred place. To create a symbiotic relationship with a place where there is a constant flow of rambling people is difficult.

Sacred places are often filled with signs, symbols, and meaningful icons. "They may appear simply decorative at first glance, they are highly potent messages to those who immerse themselves and allow inner vistas to be revealed." These markers provide expression for something much larger. They are visual imagery with directive intent. When their meaning is uncovered, the sacred place where they are held captive presents greater understanding for those within (Rebecca Hind, 2007, p. 110—English artist and sacred site researcher).

One theory of the purpose and power of sacred place is that "a place has the capacity to image microcosmically the significance of the created order as a whole." Which then proposes the question, "Can an embodied appropriation of a material context (a place) constitute an act of reference to God, or enable some sort of apprehension of God?" And, "Can the memory of events which have occurred at a particular site, including events of religious significance, be stored up and then encountered there?" (Mark Wynn, 2009, p. 15—Senior Lecturer in Philosophy and Theology, University of Oxford). If these concepts are true, the purpose of a sacred place is to encounter the world, God, history, and memory. Within these contexts, we encounter the sacred in self.

Within a sacred place we should be able to assimilate lessons learned into channeled spiritual attitudes and behaviors. If a sacred place cannot be internalized, it is merely *a place*.

Understanding Sacred Place

To understand sacred place, we need a combination of analytical thinking, synthetic thinking, and creative thinking. We must activate both the left and right hemispheres of the brain, as well as the meta-physical components of the spirit. We need

- **Intellect:** we must study and learn about a place—its structure, its purpose, its place in space;

- **History:** we must uncover a place's history—what took place there, its story;
- **Experience:** we must participate with the place physically, mentally, and spiritually; and
- **Mystery, Imagination, Enchantment:** we must allow mystery, the expanded imagination, and enchantment to help tell us the story.

We cannot prove a place is sacred, or its level of sacredness. We study it, we learn about it, we work to understand it, we feel it, we experience it, we live it, we live within it, we share it, and we share with it. Sacred places have character and personality as much as they have history. They can interact with their inhabitants, either creating, supporting, or denying human emotions. To understand a sacred place, look for its adjectives—beautiful, mystical, inspiring, enchanting, enlightening. Then seek the origin of these adjectives. What are the places' values, especially those spiritual values that create the indwelling forces that give a place its metaphysical dimensions—its sacredness? Sacred places offer something to be understood only within the ethereality of the expanded imagination. Without the meta-imagination, sacred places are only observed with visions of pleasure, as sites for tourist visits and rote rituals, not as the intimate places they are meant to be for spiritual pilgrim-participation. A sacred place is meant to channel beauty and spirit, and radiate this energy as something to behold. Within a sacred place, what good things are being held in reserve for the souls of those who enter its space?

One of the beautiful mysteries of sacred place is that it can offer us what is needed, yet utterly unanticipated, and this unrequested gift can linger long after we leave the place. What is it about a sacred place that allows it to interact with our spirit and know what we need, even if we are unaware? From first-hand experience to book knowledge, and back again. Around and around we go, to create a shift in the phenomenology of our experience until it becomes real, until we understand sacred place beyond its physical dimensions (Wynn, 2009).

Individual Importance for Sacred Place

At any place described as sacred, by one or many, something made the place sacred to someone—that something is what we must uncover to connect. If we reject that something as unbelievable, or unacceptable, it will reject us. We must work to hear the story, feel the story, see the story, experience the story which is often below the surface of the verbal account or visual observation. We do not have to agree with the story at face value as shared by someone else, but we should work to understand the story as someone else's reality. And in their reality, is there something for us to discover that has value for self and others? What does the story have to share with us and those who come after us?

If we lose a place of individual importance, we mourn the loss. When we lose a place of history where our traditions took place, we grieve. These places may be former places of worship. But they may also be places where we participated in cherished family activities on holiday, or in our daily existence. Lake cabins, mom and pop restaurants, or cheap motels of our youth; old homes we once lived in; cinder block beach houses of our summer vacations; our former schools. Places imbedded in our memory are difficult to let go of and even harder to relinquish. With the loss of these places comes the loss of a bit of their magic in our lives. A place's continued existence seems to rely on mankind. What is the fate of our sacred places?

Preserving Sacred Place

In America, we have moved away from our traditional places of worship. We tear down our historic houses of worship, we modernize them without supporting their history, we redesign them into all-purpose spaces, and in so doing we lose their comfort for our souls. In our attempts to create all-encompassing space for the masses we have traded our spiritual sanctuaries for commonplace multipurpose rooms where we play basketball, fold out chairs and tables for parties, charge the public to use this space, then create make-shift space for worshiping God on Sunday. While there is nothing wrong in creating multi-purpose places within sacred places, I personally find it most difficult to move from a physical state of thinking, into an in-spirit state of worship, in a common place more akin to a business, pub, theatre, or recreation center.

We have also become a country that too easily disposes of other types of culturally important buildings, unlike our friends in Ireland, England, France, Greece, and around the world who are still using and refurbishing buildings created a thousand years ago. We call a building of fifty-years an old building and are as likely to tear it down and rebuild as we are to remodel and preserve it.

Going to Sacred Place

People wrongfully attempt to treat sacred places as "containers for our activities" (Wynn, 2004, p. 27). Like *going to* a stadium for a ballgame, or *going to* church to be entertained by worship.

Wynn (2004, p. 27) further states that a sacred place "is not a backdrop for behavior" but a place that integrates with a person's character. We don't go there to do something, we go there to *be with*, to create a relationship. It should be like spending time with a friend, enjoying being in her presence and taking part in intimate communication.

Casey (1993, 2009) says that sacred place is more of an event than a thing to be assimilated into known categories. It is alive; it is an active participant. A place can be predictable or unpredictable. It can take us beyond, or below, our expectations. Getting to know a place requires our willingness and readiness to connect and the place's willingness to cooperate. It is like a trip with a friend where we engage each other with questions and open communication rather than voicing our pre-determined conclusions (Casey, 1993, 2009).

The difference in a place and a sacred place is that one is a location you *go to*, the other you *commune with*. A place is setting your beautiful bone china tea cups on a shelf behind glass to be viewed. A sacred place is taking them down and using them with your friends to enjoy the ritual of tea. This ritualistic use does not make the china common, like your everyday plastic dishes. This use brings out the sacred by using the tea cups in a purposeful relationship-building, life-sustaining activity.

Access to Sacred Place

While various levels of access, or lack of access, to a sacred place or degrees of the sacred within a sacred place may make it special and unique, these barriers may also create negative emotions and formulate a physical resistance to a place. Lack of access such as locked doors, screens, keep-out signs, and other barriers create psychological thresholds as well as physical ones.

A closed or locked door to a sacred place makes it simply a box to hold things, or to keep things out. An open or unlocked door is a welcome invitation to enter and participate. It says, my intimacy is yours with which to share (Bachelard, 1994).

The Body and Sacred Place

According to philosophers like Gaston Bachelard, 1920-1962—France; Friedrich Bessel, 1784-1846—Germany and Russia; and ancient-time philosophers like Plato, 428 BC-348 BC—Greece; and Aristotle, 384 BC-322 BC—Greece, the knowledge of place can be stored within the human body as well as the mind. More recent medical studies of this phenomenon refer to it as muscle memory, which may or may not be memory independent from the mind. How ever it occurs, this body-storage of knowledge and memory involves the body's ability to reproduce movements without conscious thought. This body-memory is believed to be created by and reinforced with repetitive movements, such as playing a piano, typing on a keyboard, riding a bicycle, kissing. Once the memory is emplaced, it can be recalled and reoccur in the future without conscious thought. While this memory encoding begins with cognitive activity, with time the consciousness of activity lessens to the point where the body appears to take action of its own accord.

In relating this concept to a place, especially a sacred place, consistently going to a specific place appears to increase our potential for sacred activity at that place. Our mind and our body together at a place allows for our mind and body to work more effectively in creating a relationship with any place (Bachelard, 1994). Likewise, by placing ourselves (our body as well as our mind) in close proximity to some place of historical significance, meaningful events, or close to a person(s) (either alive or dead—such as their grave, their home, their workplace), we can better connect with anything the place has to offer relating to past history, past events, or people, because of the placement of our body (Bachelard, 1994).

Wynn (2009) supports this concept and states that by going to a place repeatedly, in body (with our body), we more easily experience what the place has to offer than if we simply go to different places, or if we simply think about, or study in the pages of a book, a place within our mind.

Might these same arguments be applied to experiencing God more so with frequent visits to a specific place of worship, a building in which people throughout history have praised and worshiped God? And may we likewise experience God more so, when we go in body to worship, rather than just worshiping at home, in mind? This theory implies that a tangible connection to a place of significance, by our body's presence, offers greater rewards of expression than simply thinking about a place, an event, or a person. Thereby offering an embodied appropriation, not simply a mental appreciation.

Other studies have found that the directional positioning of a human body in relation to a place also has significant meaning. With our body, we approach a building directly, we draw away from it, we turn our back towards it, or we turn our side to it. Each position shares a message of our intended relationship with the place (Casey, 1993, 2009).

In the ultimate sense, the human body is the supreme sacred place on this earth. It was created by God, it is the temporary home of our spirit and soul, and it is the home into which God's Spirit is called to dwell. If the human body did not exist, all other places would remain nameless with no primary function. Even more so than nature, the human body is the fundamental place-creation by God and our human creations of, and interactions with, other places give each their meaning.

Globalization and Sacred Place

The modern, universal movement toward globalization, while positive in the sense that it interconnects the world allowing us to work together in ways never before possible, also presents legitimate concerns that through this interconnectivity places and their unique people and traditions may become so melted in this global pot that they drift into extinction.

History and Sacred Place

"Something that makes a place sacred could be the history behind the place. It may be a place where you feel a connection: a connection to something that is actually present or to a distant memory. These sacred places connect us to someone who we may or may not have known, but with whom we have something to share" (Ashley Bubenik, Sacred Place–Sacred Space Class, 2010).

Places are storehouses of memory and can activate a storehouse of memory in the people who visit them. These places hold on to the memory of those who visited them before, to be shared with those who follow after. The history of a place can affect current activity and current behaviors (Casey, 1993, 2009).

When we connect with the memory of a place, or the storied memory within a place, we connect with some level of unity with the people of its past through common purposes, common thoughts, common beliefs, or a common style of worship, activity, or ritual—like in a church. We find a harmony or peace with the place's history, or with the storied memory within its walls. A harmony with the past experiences held within the place and within our mind and our spirit as well as within our body and soul. Likewise, we may experience a place's history of disharmony, hate, anger, death, or offensive behavior, and share in the feelings of pain, sorrow, and despair. These inward memory-triggers share the character of those who proceeded us in occupying and participating with the place. The sensory triggers within us connect with the triggers within the place.

There are at least two views one might examine when looking at the significance of history and sacred place. One view would be that sacred places, once recognized, should remain static or unchanged to preserve that history authentically. The other view provides that mankind is always creating history, therefore sacred places should not remain static, but should represent various time periods throughout history, which includes the present—which at some point in the future will become history. This view states that each period of time should consider adding new art, new designs, or new symbols to overlay history, while yet protecting the past. It also presumes that some items should even be removed or modified (Professor Michael Tavinor in North & North, 2007, p. 35).

Obviously history is an ever-evolving process. If we only look to a distinguished past in defining sacred places, we might miss out on opportunities to create new sacred places for the future. Likewise, when modifying historic places, we might lose some aspects of the sacred significance of that place. So how do we best address these choices?

"Sacred Places come to us out of the past. They are handed on, down the centuries, so the past is where we must begin our exploration" (Feehan, in *Abbey Leix Anthology*, Volume One, 2010, p. 70). Through decades of study we have determined that many sacred places, as we know them, were the sites of previous sacred activity, atop more previous sacred activity. Dr. Feehan refers to this multi-layered history as "overlay" or the "latest layer of special meaning these places have acquired," with each generation of inhabitants adding its layer (Feehan, in *Abbey Leix Anthology*, Volume One, 2010, p. 72). In protecting the history of sacred places, we must always start with a study of the past and appropriately add our significant layers, but without negating, or hiding from discovery, the more distant past. This overlaying of history is a very difficult task, but is of vital significance in preserving, while adding to, the history of space and place.

In our attempts to connect with the sacred past of a sacred place, we must not forget to connect with its present. Without the past there is no present, but without the present, there is no future.

Culture and Sacred Place

Casey (1993, 2009) discusses place as a location, and a dimension of cultural and historic expression. Once the place and the culture join together, they should become inseparable. People in place, coming together to create the sacredness of place, through purposeful cultural intent and action.

There is great sacred value in learning about and communicating the emotions and details of one's place of origin, culture, or current habitat in uncovering the sacred places from the past, in preserving these places for the future, and in establishing new sacred places. Unless we accept the responsibility of telling our story, our place's story, these stories will eventually expire.

Architecture and Sacred Place

Historically, sacred places present an architecture that separates them from the mundane and common places that we encounter in our everyday world. Through physical and spiritual symbolism, building materials, the physics of reflecting sound waves, the use of natural light, and in their general layout for spiritual intent, they reflect a sense of the sacred in place (Thomas Barrie, 1996—AIA Professor of Architecture).

Professor, architect, and sculptor Christopher Day (2004) states that a building's construction materials each have individual qualities that strongly influence what the building has to say, especially if the building is a sacred place. Wood presents warmth. Steel is hard and cold. Stone speaks of history. And the care, or lack of care, of the building materials and of the building itself perhaps shouts louder than the voice of the physical matter.

Light is one of my favorite elements within a sacred place. It is a radiant gift to enter a sacred place and feel the sense that someone, hundreds of years ago, took the time to think about how light would cut through his stained-glass windows as long as they stood in place.

Throughout history the arrangement of sacred places within the space of nature has been dictated by their orientation to the sun, moon, stars, wind, the four directions, or any one or more of these created bodies or orders. This arrangement by directional location has passed through times of science and times of mysticism, but it continues from ancient times until today as a powerful force for the architectural design of sacred places.

Common Sacred Places

Mankind shares common sacred places, those open for communion and sharing. But, we also desire individual sacred places—multiple, or individual sacred place—singular, that may only be sacred to us or a few. Common sacred places are not common, in the sense of less value, but common in that they offer a collective community.

Some of the most common sacred places are

- graves, cemeteries, and burial grounds;
- places of purification such as sweat lodges and places of water;
- healing sites such as artesian springs;
- places where plant and animal wildlife flourish;
- places where rare animal and plant life live and grow;
- stone quarries where minerals like turquoise, quartz, obsidian, crystal, and pipestone are found;
- astronomical sites that track the movement of stars, sun, and planets including ancient medicine wheels and places like Stonehenge;
- special places from which to observe sunsets and sunrises;
- historic sites where important events took place;

- isolated places in nature such as national parks and nature conservatories.
- sites of mythical tales of legend and lore;
- places that stimulate dreaming and visions; and
- places of ancient rock carvings and petroglyphs.
  (Swan, 1990, p.p. 44-67)

Bachelard (1994) tells us that, even at these common sacred places, perceiving the sacred can be difficult. Sometimes it requires averting our attention away from the vastness of place to the minute details that arise from the nooks and crannies of the structure or location. Leonardo da Vinci often told artists who seemed overwhelmed by the expanse of a place or a project to pay close attention to the "crack in the wall ... for there is a map of the universe in the lines that time draws on these old walls" (p. 144).

Nature and Sacred Place

The creation of sacred places in nature may be our human attempts to restore the concept of the original Garden of Eden on earth, when all was well between God, man, and nature. Perhaps we find this endeavor in our own home gardens and in our magnificently groomed public gardens more so than anywhere else in nature. These glorious home grounds where we self-employ ourselves for hours on end, and these places in public where we leisurely walk and contemplate life, are places where mankind attempts to bring structure and order to the natural free-flow of nature's expanse through our organizational cultivation. I encountered this *Garden of Eden* phenomenon in Monet's Gardens in Giverny, France, which were the inspiration for many of Monet's most famous paintings, but I have also encountered it in other multi-sensory gardens throughout England, Ireland, and the United States. Well-planned gardens meet all the sensory qualities for potential sacred encounters as they have the ability to stimulate every sense. Unfortunately, we far too seldom move from our elemental appreciation for their corporal beauty, to the higher levels of sacred encounter beyond their glamour and décor.

Validating Sacred Place

One thing we know about sacred places is that people seek them out. We search for special places, specific places, unique places, places where there are people with whom we share common interests, beliefs, and goals; places that call us to come in and participate. When any of these places become known by many, they may formally and individually be ordained as a *Sacred Place*. From my research and interviews, there are indeed some places that are more conducive to sacred activity and experience than others and deserve this declaration. But, then, we must question a sacred place's validity and trustworthiness. Or must we? Is there some standard test for sacred validity, some test for the soundness of a sacred encounter? A marker for a sacred experience to be legitimate? Or is such validity an individual, meta-physical persuasion only?

According to Theology Professor Mark Wynn (2009), sacred validity is supported by two types of human beliefs, sensory beliefs and scientific beliefs. Sensory beliefs are based on personal experience, feelings, and emotions, making a sacred place a very individual and personal encounter of overtly unmeasurable phenomena. Scientific beliefs are based on facts, history, and probable evidence, making sacred place experience something that needs to be measured with a cognitive process for accountability. How do we balance these two opposing views of validity?

My theory is that phenomena like sacred places reside in a third belief category of ethereality beliefs. In this classification, sensory belief or scientific belief, literal or figurative, fact or myth, all ask the wrong questions and therefore come to wrong conclusions. If we are looking to one faction or the other within these self-limiting categories for validity, we entirely miss out on the gifts of phenomena.

Our answers for the validity of sacred encounters lie not within the physical realm, but within a realm that exists between and beyond these structural confines. The senses and science, fact and myth, can lead us to the doorway of a sacred place, but they cannot take us inside.

A true sacred place is dynamic, allowing willing participants to interact with it and within it, and through such interaction to encounter God, spirit, history, and even self. A sacred place's mere geometric structure is designed to be transcended. It acts as a shadow of something much more universal, cosmic, spiritual, and significant within, beneath, or beyond the structure. Yet, this geometric transcendence is often rejected by a logical mind seeking validity. The inner-spirit is not awakened, and the sacred place is not entered spiritually.

One unique way I have used to validate the unmeasurable quality of the sacred is simply to observe the facial and body reactions of those who enter a sacred place as they encounter whatever it has to offer them. Through their responses, the sacred may express itself more so than through any other personal sensory stimulation provided directly by the place.

Ultimately, each individual encountering a sacred place must determine its validity for self. Each sacred place speaks a language of its own and converses with whom it wishes in its own appointed time and way. We cannot apply any standard form of validity-measurement to these sacred phenomena.

Little River, Smoky Mountains National Park

Chapter Sixteen
What Is Sacred Space

Sacred space has the ability to offer an other-worldly atmosphere more so than a sacred place. Saint Thomas Aquinas (Catholic Priest, a medieval theologian, and meta-physical philosopher who lived between 1225-1274 AD) states that *existence* is a common theme shared by all living beings, in nature and mankind. If the source of this existence is God, the Master Creator of all living beings, there is a commonality in all living things that can then be felt, seen, and expressed within the atmosphere. Not everywhere in the atmosphere, but in the atmosphere of sacred space, the place where the essence of living things can unite and mutually experience each other's gifts on a meta-physical level. All creation contains this transcendent quality (Bourke, 1968).

On my way to the Smoky Mountains, I take the same route, a ritual for me, entering the gateway to the National Park by way of Route 73 from Townsend, Tennessee. This scenic road skirts alongside the Little River, offering a snakelike journey through wooded foothills leading to the beautiful historic village of Gatlinburg. Whether heat of summer, or cold of winter, I roll down my car windows, slow my pace, and listen to the water as it cascades over massive rock formations and recently fallen trees. I often stop during this crossing and walk down the bank to the water's edge, reaching down to draw out a few small rounded stones, worn smooth and glossy by the constant flow of these primal waters. It is something I just do, without cognitive thought. I have done it since my youth.

I remember one November evening's trip particularly well. My wife and I were traveling to the mountains for our annual wedding-anniversary pilgrimage and we had just passed through the familiar open park gate onto the Little River Road, when snow began to fall. These were large flakes of thin snow that resembled the cornflake cereal of my youth. The kind of cereal where I would cut small slivers of banana and drop them into the milk and cereal. Enough banana to get a taste with every bite. I can smell the bananas as I write this. The snow was falling very softly onto the warm windshield of my car, creating a sound much like the small feet of mice scampering across a wooden floor. With the windows down and the snow-chilled air rolling into my car, I could feel the contrast of the car's heater and nature's cold. I remember it as a very pleasant paradox of opposites for my senses. This was one of those evenings when you could smell and taste the weather. Time was lost for a moment, a sense of peace and awe was attained, and there was a divine presence in the atmosphere. Not a forged sense of mysticism, but a genuine impression of the sacred. What was it I was experiencing?

I have traveled this road well over one hundred times. But now, what was once an eighteen mile stretch of road and space connecting me to my intended destination, is a personal pathway, a portal into sacred place and space, at least it is for me. Almost instantly I sense the sacred in this space as I enter the park's welcoming gate. Is my experience psychological, physiological, or spiritual? Is it the hand of God, the voice of nature, enchanted and youthful memory, or storied memory in the atmosphere? I tend to think it is all these things.

Chapter 16

A sacred pathway, through the space of nature, whether traveled by foot or car, has the ability to unite our spirit, soul, mind, and body with the creation and our Creator, more so than the grandest of cathedrals. Yes, the cathedral has a power of its own, but I have determined it is often in the journey through the space that surrounds, leads to, and moves through a place, where we first encounter the sacred, and through which we are made ready to enter a sacred place. Our hearts are pricked, our spirits are awakened, and our souls are asked to come out to play. We have entered sacred space.

I am not implying that a road, even this road, is sacred in and of itself. More that pathways winding through nature can resonate with our individual spirits in very unique ways that prepare us as individuals to transition from normal routine and everyday activity, toward something special. That is the power of sacred space.

I define sacred space as a portal, a passage way, or an open expanse within which, around which, and through which energy flows or is stored and released—divine energy, spiritual or meta-physical energy, the energy of *storied memory*, and meta-sensory and meta-emotional energy. Sacred spaces are usually associated with sacred places—they surround them, flow through them, or exist within them. Sacred space may be just as implied, a space without much in the way of furnishing or the signs of man—very natural or simplistic. Or a sacred space may be very elaborate and detailed. As such, a sacred *space* may become known as a sacred *place*.

Irish culture often refers to sacred spaces as "thin-spaces," or locations where the physical and meta-physical more easily express their properties. The location of these thin-spaces can be described as unique meta-atmospheric conditions or positions where the separation of these two levels of existence are very fine and narrow—easier to penetrate. Through the existence of sacred space the spiritual world erupts into our physical world of sense perception and touches us at the level of the spirit and soul.

In my research, I conclude that it is within sacred space that the sacred and the spiritual reside and constantly flow. But, the energy that is within such a *space* benefits from a *place* to draw us in. Through the sensory expressions provided by a sacred place we enter, the thin spot is penetrated as we move from a physical to a meta-physical consciousness, and we connect with the special energy—the sacred. With this being said, I do not maintain that the sacred is confined to a particular space or spaces, or that we as people are bound by places in which we can encounter the sacred. Space and place are universal and, in so-being, access to the sacred is universal. But, as individual people, we are more apt to connect with the sacred at various individual places and spaces. There seems to be something about our particularized human composition that makes some people connect in some places and others connect in other places. We individually locate these portals in the fabric of time and space through which we as individuals connect with the sacred.

One of the detriments of our attraction to sacred place as the entry point into sacred space is that these places can sometimes hinder us, if we come to believe we must go to a particular place to encounter God, to experience the sacred. As we begin to understand sacred space, the concept that the sacred resides within space and this space flows inside and outside a place, that it flows uninhibited by physical walls or geometric barriers, we then have the ability to understand the true benefit of a sacred place as a physical to meta-physical conduit that assists the physio-psycho mind and body to transcend and interact with their counter metaphysio-psycho spirit and soul.

As we mature in our understanding of the sacred, we will still enjoy and be moved by sacred places, but we will learn to allow our spirit and soul to come out and play, work, or simply be, within most any place we find ourselves. The mind might see a place, but the spirit sees within the space of place. This enlightened sense of the sacred allows us to experience it everywhere around us. Sacred space, with its boundless immensity, becomes the very air that we breath.

Chapter 16

History and Sacred Space

When we dialog about sacred space, we are not speaking about the physical universe beyond the earth's atmosphere—outer-space. Rather, we are talking about that which surrounds, is within, and moves through sacred place. Sacred space, therefore, has a tie to sacred place-history. This then solicits the question: if the history of past events can embed itself into the memory of place, can it also embed itself into the more fluid memory of space, which seldom remains as static as place? Do historical happenings have the ability to attach to some aspect of space and travel through and within that space? Modern molecular science would tell us it is unlikely that the material molecules within air's gasses can trap sounds, smells, and other sensory data and transfer them through the atmosphere for more than brief periods of time and distance. But, we also know that dark matter and dark energy (invisible, unidentifiable, undetectable, by human instruments) make up about 95% of what we currently know (or do not know) about science, leaving a dramatic percentage of potential new scientific discoveries yet to be revealed, or forever to remain as mystery. Thus, some feature of history's potential to become embedded in space may prove to be a component of molecular science, whereby sensory information is stored in the molecules within space and held until uncovered by a sensory awakening within certain individuals.

Science, as we currently understand it, traditionally fails in pondering the consideration that other potential energy (meta-energy) resides within space and has the capability to transfer history. Ralph Waldo Emerson described this historical connection through place, space, and time as the Oversoul—an energy source comprised of spiritual essence that connects all-of-creation, throughout all-of-history. I assign individual thoughts and encounters of perceived past-life experiences within this Oversoul category, rather than the classification that some refer to as reincarnation. I maintain that our unique souls have but one life here on earth, only experiencing one body, and at the separation of body and soul at death, that soul continues its life in spirit-form in heavenly or spiritual realms, without any future physical structure or material body. However, within this Oversoul interpretation, we could easily experience a memory that was not ours. We briefly capture a touch by the wind and acknowledge a past occurrence, an old-soul experience, for which we were not physically present. If there is an Oversoul, or other universal life-essence, sacred space offers the medium for connectivity.

Another aspect of history and sacred space, similar to the Oversoul concept, is that of original Divine design. In the creation of earth and sky, of matter and space, each element contains the essence of its original Creator. That essence is forever alive and potentially active in the environment where it exists. We can therefore encounter the history of creation's story, and the Divine Creator of history, by means of the elements of space—by the flow of energy through the space of our environment, the space of our mind and body, or the space of our spirit and soul—through the space of sacred space.

In her extensive studies of Celtic culture and history, Margaret Silf (2001), an author and ecumenical Christian from the UK, states that Celtic culture has always believed in the dual realms of physical and spiritual as interwoven realities. The separation between the two realms is at times thick and impenetrable. At other times, it is thin and palpable. These thin-times allow entry into sacred space, and within this space the barriers between our physical life and eternity are lowered. We are able to find the reality present in mystery. We experience transcendence and meta-vision. We find individualized meaning in our experiences. And we are drawn into communion with ourselves, others, creation, and our Creator. Without sacred space, history would not exist.

Sacred space has a unique history of its own. It is part of an eternal flow of spiritual energy since pre-creation. The energy of God was present before time and will continue beyond time. Since the creation and until the close of man's days, mankind and all components of creation take part in this flow for our very existence. Most of the time we spend with or in sacred space is without our cognitive recognition. When we take the time to *enter* this space purposely, *in-spirit*, we gain access to new heights of meta-encyclopedic intensity and revelation.

Unlike place, sacred space is not controlled by the ebb and flow of man's desire to create, then destroy what he has made. It will forever flow within the space of a place, even if the place no longer exists.

Entranced in Sacred Space

Sacred space has the capacity to provide us with a sense of reality mixed with un-reality—meta-reality—wherein the shared encounters between a place or space and a person can occur. A sacred space is where the spiritual energy behind life moves through matter and time. This space allows us to journey into a meta-physical trance of inherent aptitudes wherein we have spiritual access to life's great questions and answers, far beyond our limited physio-psycho inherent aptitudes. This trance-like state does not present itself with emotional out-of-control expressions of stupor, for people are always in control of their spirits (I Corinthians 14:32). But Bachelard (1994) describes it more like a state of meta-physical daydream from which we can easily be brought back to reality as quickly as needed. A state from which we might flow in and out, or within which we might remain for a period of time, as desired or directed.

Words and Sacred Space

When a word enters our mind, does it simply create new thought, or does it merge with existing thought? Thought brought about by our past experiences and past knowledge with the word's meaning in relation to our mind and body, but also by the word's association with our spirit—the part of our being that super-exists our physical-being, with the capacity to access the experience and meaning, outside our cognitive or learned characteristics of recall. If so, words provide sacred pathways for connectivity to all things, with all things. Words can transport us, through their place, into sacred space.

Music and Sacred Space

One of the unique aspects of sacred space is that we can be not-here, while yet-here. To help students understand this concept, I have them listen to music. Not necessarily their favorite type of music, though it may be, but music in which we lose our sense of time and self, whether for a few seconds, or few minutes. Music that raises the hair on the arms, makes us shut our eyes, sway our head, cry, or smile. Music in which we lose sense of time and space, being swept away into the words, sounds, and vibrations. Music, perhaps beyond any other sensory stimulant, has that power to transcend the human mind to in-spirit. We are moved, yet still-here. We can also enter this transcendent state through art, poetry, or a good book. We are present in time and space, then time passes without our cognitive knowledge. This phenomenon is the in-spirit gift of sacred space.

Nooks and Crannies in Sacred Space

Bachelard (1996) encourages us never to underestimate the value and significance of "nooks and crannies" (p. viii), in helping discover the immensity of sacred space. Sacred space often likes to express itself to mankind through intimate, miniature detail. This detail may be within our favorite reading nook, in a small corner in the room of our home, in quietness under our favorite tree, in our garden, in a poem or story, or in the form of miniature images placed before our minds or spirits. We should never busy ourselves in such a way that we miss the poetry in small spaces laid out before us every day.

Uninterrupted Heavenly Space as Sacred Space

In the Genesis account of creation, Moses speaks of God separating the waters above from the waters below, water noted as present either in the pre-creation or before the beginning of the story of the first day. The separational element addressed in Genesis is often referred to as firmament, or as an expanse, but it can also be translated as *uninterrupted space*. This expanse is discussed multiple times in the Genesis account of creation, with obvious differences in meaning throughout. Sometimes it relates to *heaven*—singular, sometimes to *the heavens*—plural. The application of multiple meanings of this uninterrupted space throughout Genesis implies that more than one level or realm of the heavens exists.

We can comfortably assume that one of these levels is the atmosphere of sky, clouds, and air—the elements most closely tied to earth's functions; and one is likely the abode of God—the highest heaven sometimes referred to as the third heaven. The middle realm is typically described as outer-space. But what if level one comprises all the sky including those elements of outer-space like the stars, sun, moon, and planets since they shine their light on and share their functions with the earth? And what if the uninterrupted middle space, level two of these heavenly realms, is sacred space? The uninterrupted space, separated by a veil or curtain between the earth and its sky and the original heavenly realm? The space where the physical and spiritual come together in a continuous flow of in-between space?

If so, this uninterrupted space of sacred-space is not the spiritual realm of God and His angels, or of Satan and his angels, although scriptures tell us that a light-side of the spiritual realm and a dark-side of the spiritual realm both exist and are the places where these two opposing entities dwell. Holy angels reside with God in the highest heaven. Satan and fallen angels dwell within the dark-realm, sometimes referred to a lake of fire or a land of darkness. This dark realm was not likely to have been created during the time of the original creation, during the chronicled story of creation, because there was no need for such a place in the beginning. There was no original need for a place for saints and sinners, holy angels and fallen angels, because this separation from God by a change in the character of some created beings had not yet occurred. Satan and other angels had not yet turned against God, and man had not yet sinned or died a physical death. Therefore, there was no need for a preliminary place for these to dwell separately. This new realm was likely not created until such a place was needed after the fall of Satan and mankind (Genesis 3, II Peter 2:4, Jude 1:6, Revelations 20:10-14).

God and His angels can reach out to us from their heavenly realm. They can enter our physical world from their heavenly world and touch us, stir us, and teach us, but to move us within our very heart and soul, we must also enter their world of sacred space. Mankind needs sacred space to encounter God completely. We meet God in interrupted sacred space and it is there we must seek to find Him.

Satan, his angels, and evil spirits also reach out to us from their dark-realm. It is with these entities that our spiritual battles occur—battles against spiritual forces in this unseen, dark-realms (Ephesians 6:12), not from within the original uninterrupted space of sacred space.

This speculation or personal pondering may or may not be a provable interpretation of the firmament, expanse, or uninterrupted space formed during the creation, a space that somehow separated the earth and sky from the heavenly bodies. Accurate or not, it does not contradict the concept of a sacred space where the spiritual and physical realm come together in an in-between flow of space. Throughout the texts of Old and New Testament writers, we repeatedly hear of the realms of the physical and spiritual, and man's interaction with and between these realms through the Biblical principle of in-spirit—a word I use to represent being in spirit, doing something in spirit, or being with someone in spirit. I maintain that our spirit and soul exist in sacred space within our body, but this space also flows throughout God's creation. With our mind and our body we can enter this space and join with our spirit and soul. This spiritual state of being is *in-spirit*. In-spirit, we are able to accomplish whatever we do in spirit and in truth. We encounter ourselves, our world, and our creator on a meta-physical level.

"Between every separate thing there exists another world, an invisable world where all this separation and distance is embraced. This space between seems empty to the eye; yet to the imagination it is vibrant with pathways toward beauty. This sacred space has a latent grandeur" (O'Donohue, *Divine Beauty*, 2004, p. 242).

In-spirit in Sacred Space

In-spirit, we can be with someone in spirit (I Corinthians 5:3), worship in spirit (John 4:23-24), pray in spirit (I Corinthians 14:15), sing in spirit (I Corinthians 14:15), gain knowledge in spirit (I Corinthians 2:4), rejoice in spirit (Luke 1:47), and be provoked in spirit (Acts 17:16)—all referring to capabilities of our human spirit. These are not metaphorical statements about spirit, but are a spiritual reality in which the spirit of man participates in life. Mankind can also acquire the Spirit of God to come and live within the human body and soul where He guides us and testifies on our behalf before our Maker (John 14:16, Romans 8:9-16, I Corinthians 2:12).

We encounter enchantment in-spirit. We encounter sacred place in-spirit. And we encounter in-spirit in sacred space. The action of in-spirit takes place where the mind and the spirit, the body and the soul connect and work their inspirational and transcending magic. The place where we are in spirit is the space where the physical joins the spiritual. In the thin spots. In the tri-composition network of man and God, heaven and earth, man and creation. Sacred space is in the flow of in-between, in the ethereality beyond our ordinary perception. If we fail to encounter the sacred it is because we live too far on the fringes of our physical existence. We meet our spirit, our soul, our God, in the thin-space of in-between, not on the fringes. This sacred space runs throughout us and all of creation, making it possible for us to enter and connect with our Maker. If we can step past the physical façade and whisk away the thin veil that separates the two realms of physical and spiritual, we enter a landscape of enchanted reality—we enter sacred space.

When Saint Paul said he had learned to be content in whatever circumstances he was in, wherever he was, with whatever he had or did not have, it was because Paul had learned how to live his life in-spirit, in sacred space (Philippians 4:11).

Sacred space is where essence and spirit are found. To the human eye, this essence and spirit are often elusive, but we have the ability to slip through this physical façade that veils the sacred and "dwell for a while in the vicinity of this essence" (O'Donohue, *Divine Beauty*, 2004, p. 181).

Worship in Sacred Space

Worship is one of the most traditional forms of entering sacred space. Through our spirit-rituals, we are transported into in-spirit. While we benefit from a sacred place, like a temple, church building, or other place of worship, my research suggests that sacred space is the more potent of the two. Since sacred space exists everywhere within the flow of creative energy, it does not matter where we worship God—it can occur anywhere. Places of worship are more about places dedicated to worshipful activity, where we as humans can more readily enter sacred space, but these places of worship are not required and of themselves do not hold any holy power. It is within sacred space that holy power flows. In worshiping God, we want to raise ourselves up into holy and sacred space where God's Spirit can direct and intercede for our spirit. This sacred space is the place we worship in spirit and truth, because God is there in the space with us. This sacred space may or may not be within a place. I wish to emphasize that this does not deny the benefit of a sacred place where mankind can more easily enter the thin-space of the sacred, I simply wish to indicate that sacred space is where true worship occurs, in-spirit.

Place within Sacred Space

Our world is a place within a space. Our country, a place within our world. Our state, a place within our country. Our city, a place within our state. Our home, a place within our city. The common thread is that space connects them all. Space is the spiritual and physical connection between all places.

When we place an item into a space, that item has a tendency to become the center of the space within which it is placed. Too many items in a space, and the space loses our attention. Sacred space can get lost when we become overwhelmed by place. We must return our focus to the poetry of space (Bachelard, 1994).

While sacred place holds an important role in our transitioning from mind to spirit, it is sacred space we must enter to encounter the ethereality of our God, our self, and our world. The objective of sacred place and sacred space is to work in unison to accomplish this eternal mission.

McGavock Family Cemetery, Franklin, Tennessee

Chapter Seventeen
Sacred Sites: Sacred Places and Sacred Spaces

ithin familiar places and spaces, sometimes the sacred can be found just below the mundane, underneath the ordinary, or within the familiar. While the place or space may appear common, upon deeper observation and study, a site may reveal its sacredness, or a new degree of sacredness may be created. It is, however, often confusing to determine if the sacredness lies in the place or in the space of a given site. For this section I discuss this union of these two terms—sacred places and sacred spaces—as *Sacred Sites*.

Sacred sites cannot be understood and explained within the physical realm alone, yet we often try to relegate their phenomena to the physical and visual domain of matter. In reality, sacred sites are a spiritual phenomenon encountering a physical phenomenon. Though the collaboration of these unique, sometimes opposing realities, the sacred can be revealed within the space of a place. The physical matter of place can act as a vessel for sacred activity, but without a spiritual presence, without a spiritual thread running through or within the space of place, any activity taking place within provides a psycho-physio experience only and its potential benefits are significantly restrained. This pseudo-sacred experience is much more common than true sacred encounters, resulting in short-lived comfort, but no enduring stability. The pseudo-sacred may persuade the participant to return again and again to a proposed sacred site in search of a greater experience that may never come. Or it may create a state of disappointment in which the disheartened participant ends the search.

Sacred Sites

Can a sacred site provide an actual entry point into a meta-physical dimension or does the place or space merely act as a representation, image, or metaphor for meta-physical activity? And can a sacred place or space enter the activity that occurs at a site or does it merely set the mood for activity to take place (Wynn, 2009)?

I contend that a sacred site can offer intelligible content which can elevate our unconscious thinking to a level of consciousness, our mindful thinking to a level of spirit-thinking, and our body-action to a level of soul-activity. These places and spaces allow us to transcend the physical into the spiritual. To move from mind and body to spirit and soul. It is more than a mere metaphor, it is an actual meta-physical transition. The place and space interact with our human entities as we interact with them. We participate together in activity beyond our physical restrictions.

Sites—places and spaces—that are truly sacred, are empowered by an invisible force or source. These places and spaces of sacred power may be churches, sweat lodges, places in nature, grand cathedrals, or cemeteries; places not typically described as places or sites such as words in a book or poem, or notes in a song or musical piece;

or a variety of other places within spaces or spaces within places. As we open ourselves to the source exhibited within these sites, we begin to see glimpses beyond the physical/meta-physical barrier. That which was once secret is unveiled. Sometimes it is seen in its grandeur, but most often it is viewed through small windows of vision. Moments in time, in the sacred space of a place. This process of sacred vision can have an altering effect on thought and action for those who enter or participate with the site—a change from mental consciousness to spiritual awareness, from sacred place to sacred space. The most significant element in a sacred place is sacred space.

The Mystery in Sacred Sites

The history of a sacred site is often steeped in mystery, and this mystery is based on a bit of legend and myth mixed with fact. How do we distinguish between these historic qualifiers? Are they opposites, or do they can work in harmony to help us understand the mystery of a sacred site? Facts offer meaningful details of a site's past, but, alone, they tend to dull the senses and create immemorable experiences. Myth, legend, and mystery force us to think outside our self-limiting rote cognition in search of something new, something beyond the common place. As we tap into the mystery of a place, we tap into the mystery of the sacred flowing through it. It requires additional work in uncovering the truth within a site's mystery, but in the search for this truth, we encounter experiences with the site that we would not otherwise have encountered. If we can get to the soul of the myth, we uncover truth.

The Details of Sacred Sites

What do the details (especially the fine details) have to do with a sacred place or space? If these details are not appropriate, if they are not orderly or if they do not correctly represent the place or space, thy do not adequately serve their purpose for sacred intent, in which case they can negatively stimulate the senses and turn people away.

If they are orderly, clean, unique, and personal, if they show life and energy, they are welcoming to those who enter. The entrance to a sacred site should prepare those who enter for what is about to occur. The interior should engage us to participate. The external and internal presentation of a sacred site should let us know that we are about to enter and take part with a place that is special, a place where something out of the ordinary is going to occur.

Describing Sacred Sites

Sacred sites offer a dramatic narrative filled with timeless words of unbounded energy. But this narrative is often difficult to decode and translate into the verbal communication of everyday words.

One mistake we make in trying to describe sacred sites is in using traditional adjectives and common descriptive language in depicting what we see with our eyes. Yet each sacred site speaks a language of its own, with its own dialects. The ethereality of a sacred site can only be described through an antropocosmic understanding of the physical and the meta-physical in their co-creation correspondence with man, nature, and God as they interact with place and space. If we give our full attention to this language we can connect with the source of the language. It is only within the spiritual thread that weaves this intertwined relationship that we can appropriately understand the language of place and space, then acquire the right words to describe them. We untangle the primitive meaning of each word, one by one, and create a new language accessible for descriptive presentation and understanding. Within these words, we find keynote moments for new knowledge and sacred enchantment.

Examples of Sacred Sites and their Original Purposes

- Hermit caves and places in nature for those seeking solitude, nature, seclusion from the world, quietness, and peace. Places to contemplate, ponder, worship, and pray.

- Community places like churches, holy wells, cathedrals, temples, and other places and spaces that originally brought people together to connect with God, self, and others into a community of like-mindedness and support. These were gathering places for people. Sites where rituals transpired, healings occurred, baptisms took place, and singing, food, and fellowship flourished.

- Gravesites and cemeteries as places of memory, places to touch the past, places to contemplate mortality (life and death), quiet places to be alone or with loved ones, places to honor the dead, places of peace away from the chaos of life, places to cry, places to say hello or goodbye.

- Historic activity sites connected people with something important from their past or from the past of others with whom they had some type of relationship. Places to activate memory or create new meaningful knowledge and new memory. Places to contemplate the future based on past activity whether good or bad. Places to consider needed changes. Places to recognize and honor people of the past who had an influence on the present.

- Personal sacred sites were often in homes, local churches, vacation sites, work places, and multiple sites in nature. Places to ponder, pray, cry, study, worship, contemplate, relax, unwind, read, write, create art, be alone, or be with a small group of loved ones.

The Mind and Body's Connection to Sacred Sites

Much of the research about the mind and body and their relationship to the sacred, including their proximity of placement, suggests they both interact with place and space. While our mind and spirit create thought, emotion, and imagination, they are more drawn to the sacredness of space. The body and soul, as our physical and metaphysical structures, are more drawn to sacred place. These four categories of human existence—mind, body, spirit, soul—create a need for both sacred place and sacred space in achieving our complete human potential. The placement of the human body in a sacred place appears to hold similar value to that of placing the mind into the in-spirit state achieved in sacred space. The most physical to meta-physical transcended states occur when both mind and body take part.

What Occurs at Sacred Sites

The sense of sacredness within a sacred site can motivate people to start doing what they should be doing and stop doing what they should not be doing. Sacred sites assist in our ability to overcome addictions, renew vows of faithfulness, or reduce depression. In addition to the sacred site itself, the power source for behavior modification is also provided by the people overseeing a sacred place, and the people participating in the place now and in the past. An atmosphere of people of like minds and unity in the past and present can change a place forever. A place where there were/are a significant number of people of like minds, working together, provides even more power.

Additionally, there is power provided by the spirit of place or space, or the spirit within a place or space positioned there by God, the Spirit of God, nature, the spirit of people of past (*storied memory and history*), or people of present. This essence of spirit can be experienced within and through simplicity, grandness, visuals, words, colors, symbols, and innumerable inspirational objects. But, the actual experience takes place in the sacred space of place.

Typical sacred site occurrences include these experiences:

- ritualistic activity takes place;
- the physical senses are aroused;
- God or spiritual essence is revealed;

Chapter 17

- the spirit, soul, mind, and body unite;
- healings take place;
- people find a sense of balance and peace;
- commitments and vows are made;
- people are inspired, motivated, encouraged; and/or
- honor is bestowed upon past events and people.

What do we hope will occur at a Sacred Site? That "an echo of memory, a whisper out of our collective conscious" or something from our physical/meta-physical make up and pre-past, will arise to the surface through certain sensory and meta-sensory stimulation, and our spirit and soul will awaken (Feehan, *The Sacredness of Place* article).

Our expectations for what can happen at a sacred site deeply affect what indeed takes place. If our expectations are high, we may encounter the sacred, the pseudo-sacred, or encounter nothing at all. We cannot force true sacred experience, and a particular site does not always provide a definitive response. One of the great phenomena of sacred place and space is that when we believe a particular place will provide a sacred encounter, it often does not. Our faith in a place does not always coincide with our ability to enter the sacred space of place and move from mind and body to spirit and soul.

Elements Common to Sacred Sites

Time and again, the elements common to sacred sites offer a connection of the earth with the sky, the physical with the spiritual, or man with God through various contributions presented by nature. We are particularly drawn to things that vertically make this connection—standing or upright stone, steeples, mountains, trees, burial mounds, stairs, walls, statues, and other things that reach upward (Hines, 2007).

Dr. John Feehan (*Abbey Leix Anthology*, Volume One, 2010) agrees with Hines, stating that mankind seeks out nature in his attempts to find the sacred. Feehan's experiential research took him to sources of flowing water, water bubbling from the ground, natural wells, holy wells, wooded places, high places, places of ancient trees, primeval forests, bogs, clearings ringed by trees, open spaces, natural landscapes, places of natural beauty, standing stone (stone high crosses, standing pillars, mass rocks, and other stone memorials), and various other elements formed by, or created from, nature. Places created by creation and history.

In my personal visits to sacred sites, I have also witnessed these sacred ties to nature's elements. I have experienced waterfalls and bodies of water like creeks, rivers, lakes; pictographs and petroglyphs; ancient rock and stone art; standing stone monuments and stone crosses; solar calendars that mark the seasons; burial grounds and cemeteries; old ruins and ancient relics; mounds and circles of earth; caves; open space; bogs; mountains; wild plant and animal life; wooded forests; mystical silence; and offerings of tobacco, sage, flowers, grain, food, or prayer ties left behind by visitors.

Ritual is a universal cornerstone for sacred activity. Common elements for ritual include prayer, song, dance, meditation, smudging, the burning of incense, sacrifices or offerings, going to water, sacred pipe or smoke ceremonies, sweats, rituals with fire, purification rituals, oaths, and dedications. These rituals are formed around special days, times, seasons, and places in solitude, in small groups, or with large groups. For most people, a ritual is simply an orderly sequence of activity with or without a sense of heightened consciousness. When visiting a culture different from our own, we are often asked to view or participate in these rituals, although one sign of authenticity is when a culture reserves some rituals for members of the culture only. Group participation is often nothing more than a means for tourist promotion. Authentic spirit-rituals are different. They are generally not a part of tourist activity, but are offered within more intimate settings. They may be planned or spontaneous responses to sacred encounters at a sacred site. Being personally asked to participate in a cultural ritual after or outside a traditional tourist event is to be understood as an honor. These are the rituals where sacred activity is more like to occur.

Mankind also creates his own spiritual signs, symbols, and elements for sacred activity. These elements may appear as decoration, such as Native American medicine wheels or dreamcatchers, but in their original context they may offer messages to those who immerse themselves and allow inner vision to be revealed (Hines, 2007).

Likewise, there should be non-tangible elements common to sacred sites such as a connection to a specific person or people who formally lived there, or an event in history that occurred there, an unexplained existence or presence, the supernatural, a good or bad memory attached to the site, or a good or bad memory attached to one's personal past and activated by contact with a site.

Hines (2007) notes that sacred sites have active and resting phases, meaning that even though the elements are present, as individuals we may not always be able to connect or be touched by the sacred presence at a site.

History and Sacred Sites

There is a sacred world that existed before, waiting to be revealed in the present and the future. A history in the land, in a place, in a space, in our mind or body, or in our spirit or soul. Sacred places and spaces can share that history or unleash it from its place within our human form. Whether this history resides within matter around us, matter within us, or in the spiritual flow of energy through the space within and between matter, the sacred offers a porthole for connection to a sacred lesson of history that speaks to our very peculiar souls.

Within the flow of memory at a sacred site is held the history of times long passed. Some memories will be transmitted to one individual alone, some will to be transmitted to a few, some to many. But some memory will always remain in holding without future revelation of understanding. It is forever present to stir the human soul.

Sacred places and spaces are frequently the sites where saints and spiritual people lived, worked, and died, and places where significant historical events took place. The sites themselves retain an identity of the place's history. While the objects buried or left behind at these sites may have their meaning in their inhabitant's simple everyday struggles to sustain life, they may likewise express spiritual meaning—or perhaps both. They can be symbols clothed in the ordinary, yet full of mystery (Feehan, in *Abbey Leix Anthology, Volume One*, 2010). By examining the items unearthed at historical sites, we get to know the people who were there before us, and sometimes in our examination of these people, we see ourselves and our future. Visiting museums, reading historic journals and manuscripts, touring historic homes and landscapes, traveling abroad, walking in nature, discussing the past with our elders, or taking part in an archeological dig can open our physical and psychological processes to the sacred mystery that is often just below the surface—the mystery, in history. This mystery in history can then open our spiritual processes to that which is even deeper beneath the surface.

When initially surveying a sacred historic site, we must first step back and examine the big picture where the more obvious elements of the sacred reside. We can accomplish this by researching historical data—including details of what the original landscape looked like; examining old and recent photos of the site; locating historic sketches or paintings; or reading stories, letters, or journals noting the details of the site during its past. We need to be able to recreate,

Chapter 17

if only in our minds, the way the original site appeared, as well as observing how it looks today. Even more beneficial is the process of re-creating, through new sketches or models, what the area, piece of land, or buildings formerly looked like. Progress may have greatly altered the landscape or various facets of the landscape. The site may have been an open field or wilderness at one time, a current building may have originally faced a different direction, or have been moved to the location at a time well after any significant historical activity took place. Or perhaps an important structure is now missing. These changes may have opened the sacred to be more readily visible, or they may have covered over various components of a location's sacred past. In attempting to observe the authenticity of a sacred place or space it is imperative to allow history to tell us the true story and how that story has changed since the conception of the site. We can become so focused on a sacred place and its elements that we fail to examine it in its full context—historically and currently. Often the potency of a sacred place is found in understanding its history and in examining the space around the place. That potency may be grassed over, built over, or overlayered in a variety of ways.

History and the Future of Sacred Sites

Another aspect of sacred sites and history relates to the role history plays for the future. If history identifies a site as sacred, is it once sacred, always sacred? Can a sacred place or space lose it sacredness or can a non-sacred place or space become sacred based on newly un-covered information? Who has the right to decide? Is it the professional historian, the amateur history buff, the historic preservationist, politicians, religious leaders, or the current generation of people living and desiring to use the space in some manner that may or may not support its past?

Many historic and sacred sites have been ruined, or concealed, at least temporarily, through modern attempts to modify, update, revitalize, progress, or even preserve or restore. Without careful intervention and a thorough knowledge and understanding of a site and its relevant history, a sacred site can easily be destroyed in a misconceived effort to change it into something perceived to be better (Hind, 2007).

Place Names and Sacred Sites

Dr. Feehan (2003) tells us that quite often the name of a place gives us a clue to its historic past, its story. Does the name imply that groves of trees once were present, or acres of woodland? Was this a past place of worship, a hillside, waterfall, a town, or garden? Is there a connection to a famous person from long ago? This something or someone may no longer be visually present, but at one time played a crucial role in the site's importance. The name of a sacred site very likely tells us the first paragraph of the site's story.

Likewise, when we give the name sacred to a site we are stating this is a place with unique purpose, a place where God's work is emphasized or where activities and rituals are conducted with sacred intent.

Sacred Sites: Power by Association

Sacred sites of old were often places and spaces where common practical necessities were readily accessible like shelter, water, food, and ready defense. They were also places where various sensory attractions called to one's soul, that offered a connection between man, God, and nature, that echoed the pulse of God. In these places and spaces God's presence could easily be sensed through His creation. Some of the earliest sacred sites were holy wells, burial grounds, earth mounds, temples, churches, and monasteries. Most of them were sites located in nature. These were places of solitude, quietness, and simplicity wherein was an openness of communication with nature and God.

From these early places, people then began to create sacred places and spaces via association with people, places, and spaces from the past and the historical events surrounding these people, places, and spaces. This connection could also be seen in the re-creation of form and style in the sacred buildings that followed.

Current modern day sacred sites are still marked by this same sacred association—their power by association or extension to other similar places and spaces from the past. Nature, animal life, trees, water, and other traditional aspects of creation are frequent elements of sacred site design, because in nature we can easily see God's hand in creation. But also to similar houses of worship from the past because they were the archetype houses of worship. This power of association includes relics left behind from a place's history. Tangible and intangible relics from when and where monks, priests, saints, and people of ordinary lives lived, worked, communed, worshiped, and even played. In our attempts to connect though an association with these people and places of old, we hope to reconnect with God and our world as it was intended to be.

Preserving Sacred Sites

How do we make appropriate use of a sacred site or potential sacred site's obvious and unknown resources to advance knowledge, understanding, and life-quality? How do we allow the many to enjoy a site, without exploiting the site and the people who reside, or formally resided, in the area of the site—such as setting aside formally private areas of land for national parks and nature sanctuaries while controlling the negative effects of the masses of people who will then visit these sites? How do we use a site, without exploiting this usage? What is the balance between appropriate human utility and destruction?

Modernizing older church buildings is a perfect example of exploitation. While modern conveniences can be wonderful additions to an old church, the way these updates are made can have a significant effect on the space's continued sense of the sacred. We can honor or dishonor memory and history by altering a place in any offensive way (Casey, 1993).

Inappropriate manipulation of sacred places and spaces may not always be by intent. Repainting with a modern color that is historically incorrect, replacing historic windows to conserve energy, removing walls to create open space, cutting down trees to expose a structure, removing historic gardens for walkways, or adding carpet atop original wooden floors for comfort (worse yet, removing old wood floors) may be well-meaning, but they all influence the history of place and space and thus influence the sacredness provided through such history or *storied memory*. Not all changes are bad and without change we would not have many of the benefits of today's modern conveniences for our homes, our land, or our places of worship. We appreciate added amenities such as restrooms and heating and cooling to any site we might frequent. But a reverence toward history must strategically be pursued in our modification. An appropriate preservation mentality must be acquired and employed to lessen the damaging destruction often placed upon our diminishing sacred place and spaces in the name of physical progress and growth.

Preserving the Presence in Sacred Sites

Is visiting and studying sacred places simply a hobby, an archaeological or visitor attraction, or is there deeper meaning in what can be observed and uncovered (Feehan, *The Sacredness of Place* article). Dr. Feehan argues that a true sacred place provides not simply an atmosphere, but a presence. With time and lack of attention, or inappropriate preservation, a place can lose that presence (Feehan, *The Sacredness of Place* article).

Let's discuss the concept of *presence* for a moment, because the preservation of a presence is a much deeper concept than the simple preservation of a place. A presence implies that something is here with us. It is not simply an atmosphere conducive to something happening, rather something is present that creates the atmosphere. Something exists to be uncovered. So, while multitudes of people experience a *sense* of the sacred, very few uncover the cause and experience the meaning behind the atmosphere, and therefore, never experience a true connection with the sacred through this presence.

While it is important to pay close attention to the atmosphere of a sacred place to be able to preserve that atmosphere, it is more important to connect with and preserve the source of that atmosphere, or we are likely to modify the atmosphere to accommodate people's desires and pre-conceived notions of what the place should represent. For more than sixty years during the mid-20th century, the Eastern Band of the Cherokee portrayed the Cherokee people by adorning themselves with full headdresses and standing next to teepees, neither of which are true examples of the historical Cherokee people. Why this inaccurate presentation? Because that was what the non-Cherokee tourists expected. By meeting the perceived needs and ideas of the public, much of the more sacred aspects of the Cherokee culture were hidden for an extended period of time, and some components were lost forever. This culture has learned from its mistakes and over the past fifteen years has begun to remove inappropriate representations of their historic culture, taking part once again in ancient cultural activities. They are also utilizing modern technology and modern thinking to determine which historic aspects of the culture are the most important to pass on to their children and the public and which should give way to progress.

Sacred places have the same vulnerability, even in our efforts to preserve them. We cover up something because it seems distasteful or politically incorrect. We adapt something to meet perceived needs or desires (such as comfort or entertainment value). Or we change terminology in order not to offend. While addressing these types of concerns is appropriate, we must avoid making hasty, poorly researched, politically motivated decisions as we care for places we call sacred. We must learn to leave historical layers in place, add authentic new layers appropriately, and consider intensely the past and the present and any future consequences of our altercative actions. If a sacred place loses it presence, its true sacredicity will be lost. No matter how hard we try to construct a sacred presence through an unauthentic atmosphere, we will fail.

Access to Sacred Sites

When a fee is charged to enter, or limitations are placed on who can and cannot enter a sacred site, these barriers tend to affect negatively the opportunity of a potential encounter. While some pleasure may be derived from these type of sacred site visits, they often remain as subsensory stimulation at the most.

While medieval churches and sacred places of worship did not charge a fee to enter, they did not allow all worshipers and visitors to see all the site had to offer. These places were divided into sacred spaces and sacred levels with doors, curtains, and screens between each. These barriers may have had the intent of creating a desire to see beyond, or in even forcing a place's recognition as sacred for those who beheld it, but they also annoyed those refused entry.

For five years, I taught a college course titled *Exploring Spirituality in Sacred Place and Sacred Space.* We visited holy wells, historic churches and cathedrals; cemeteries and ancient burial site; historic Indian villages, mounds, and ceremonial grounds; waterfalls and virgin forestland; wilderness areas; the remains of old castles; former places where monks lived and worked; the list continues. Notations of merit always made by my students related to whether or not a site was accessible, if there was a fee to enter the site, if the place was locked or otherwise unavailable for entry, or if a portion of the site was unavailable for entry by everyone. One of my activities was to take students to the most historic church in Franklin, Tennessee, which is open twenty-four hours a day. At the site, we opened the door and walked in to experience the place—free and open to all. Then we walked nearby to another historic church and I asked one of the students to go ahead and open the door for the others. When she turned the door handle, the door would not open—it was locked. We then sat outside the church for a few moments and talked about how they felt about one church being open to everyone, twenty-four hours a day, and another being open only at specific times. Their comments were always the same—the sacred should be accessible to everyone.

We had the same discussions with students in Ireland and in England when we had to pay to enter a cathedral or other place noted as a sacred site. The feelings were the same. Why should one have to pay to observe that which is sacred? Initially, I agreed with the students. In theory, I still do. However, I have begun to understand better the significant cost in preserving a historic or sacred site for future generations. A measured balance should be attained such as free-entry days each month so that those seeking more of a sacred experience have a choice.

Pilgrimages to Sacred Sites

As humans, we are pilgrims in the world, weary one day, happy the next, walking through our physical existence from our immemorable past to our uncharted future. To enter or return to a significant sacred site alters this course forever.

In pilgrimages, we are generally following another's path to find our own. We are moving our body through space to get to a place where we can transcend or otherwise find meaning in our journey and destination. Sometimes it is important to define our own pilgrimage by allowing ourselves to be called to new places and seek after new adventures, places with no connection to our past, only to our future.

One of the most traditional forms of pilgrimages was developed in the earliest centuries when Jewish people made an annual pilgrimage to the site of the original temple in Jerusalem. Pilgrimages then continued for Christian people to sites of Old and New Testament importance, especially to the sites where Jesus and Christian saints lived, visited, ministered, and performed miracles. The area known as the Holy Land, between the Jordan River and the Mediterranean Sea—the land now of Israel and Palestine—is often noted as a place for sacred site pilgrimages. Pagan and druid worship may have also had their pilgrimages, but their journeys to sacred sites are not as strongly supported by recorded history as those of Judaism, Christianity, and Islam. What we do have is left to historical interpretations through oral stories and includes pilgrimages to stone circles, astronomical sites, ancient tombs, and labyrinths (North and North, 2007).

Some Christians find it challenging to accept the concept of sacred places and spaces and the perceived human need for pilgrimages to these sites, because of Jesus' statement recorded in the Gospel book by the Apostle John. Jesus said that a time would come when the place of sacred worship would no longer mattered. "An hour is coming when neither in this mountain nor in Jerusalem will you worship the Father" (John 4:21, New American Standard Bible). "God is Spirit and those who worship Him must worship in spirit and truth" (John 4:24, New American Standard Bible). Add to these words the idea of an Omnipresent God who can be at all places at all times, and a Christian could conclude that no places or spaces are sacred, therefore of no benefit for Christian pilgrimages.

After much pondering, I challenge this conclusion. I would argue that through God's omnipresence He can indeed be present and accessible in any place. Therefore, if we chose a particular place to worship God or to which we make a pilgrimage, He is surely there. And with Jesus' emphasis on worshiping in spirit and in truth rather than place, I contend that worshiping in spirit and truth takes place in-spirit, and in-spirit occurs in sacred space. Jesus' discussion was not a debate about place, but an argument about what should occur in worship, an in-spirit activity, not rote ritual. It is not about the "going to" as in going to church. It is about what is to happen when we go and when we arrive, wherever that place might be. Each week Christians and others around the world go to their personal places of worship, places we usually call churches or temples, and there we conduct sacred worship. Is this not a pilgrimage application of the sacred to place and space?

My research indicates that within the genetic make-up of human beings is a need for place. This research also indicated that we as humans need to journey to designated sacred sites to help us distinguish the sacred from the mundane. North and North (2007) came to the same conclusion, stating that our visits to sacred sites give us examples of the sacred to take back to our homes, our churches, and our ordinary lives. Without them, we do not know what the sacred looks like.

Henry David Thoreau (*Walking*, 2005) presents another form of pilgrimage, walking in nature. It is not about a destination at which you are to arrive, but about the place where you are at any given moment during a walk. The journey and the places discovered along the way are the pilgrimage. If we focus on the place ahead, we miss out on the journey. Thoreau also separates this adventurous walking from walking for exercise. Exercise may be a by-produce of walking, but the walk itself is about something much more sacred. Thoreau liked to call this type of waking, sauntering. The intent for sauntering is to remove us from society and its confining institutions into a world of fields and trees and water and beauty. Its purpose is to engage the human spirit and soul as much as the human mind and body. If we walk a mile and are still thinking about work or home, or anything other than thought aroused by the walk, we have not yet begun the pilgrimage.

Two types of pilgrimage on which I take students in my sacred place and sacred space classes are vision quests and object quests.

For vision quests, the students walk in nature until something seems to call to them, to gain their attention. The students then sit down and pay attention to the item, often journaling their findings and thoughts. They might also select a small plot of ground (approximately three foot by three foot) for their study. Their pilgrimage takes place by a thorough examination and journaling of all the elements within this space, both atop and beneath the earth. My most common object quests are for feathers or small colorful stones; specific types of birds, flowers, trees, or edible wild plants; or animal tracks or even animal scat.

Personal Sacred Sites

As I have journaled my sacred site moments over the years, I noted the following places to be my most personal sacred sites. These are places where I find it the easiest to enter the thin-space of sacred space: on my screened back porch with tree and hilltop views in nature; in one of the simple old churches in Cades Cove with open windows and wooden pews; in the Great Smoky Mountains National Park; at my Copper Creek cabin where I stayed when working on the Cherokee Indian Reservation; at one of the quaint cottages at the Buckhorn Inn in Gatlinburg, Tennessee; in a historic graveyard in Leiper's Fork, Tennessee; in a historic whitewashed church in Franklin, Tennessee; in the sanctuary of St. Michael and All Angels Church in Abbeyleix; in Heywood Gardens, the Slieve Bloom Mountains, or the Rock of Dunamase in County Laois, Ireland; at Harris Manchester College, University of Oxford; at the old Lighthouse Motel in Gulf Shores, Alabama; in the thought-provoking words bound in books by Emerson, Thoreau, or Bachelard; in a light English manor house mystery; in the music of jazz musician Sidney Bechet or a piece of Baroque music; in the private moments of my morning cup of Irish Tea or my social moments with a cigar at the Oxford Men's Club or James J. Fox Cigar Merchants in London; at the old home places of my grandparents, in West Tennessee; special times with my wife, children, and grandchildren; and in the seasonal changes of spring or fall. I have encountered sacred space in all

Chapter 17

of these places. Many are examples of sacred sites accessible to all. Some are ornamental in detail; some are very simplistic. Personal sacred sites come in all forms.

Creating or Re-Creating Sacred Sites

To create or recreate a sacred site, the process begins with a knowledge of the qualities that offer the opportunity to be in-spirit, the qualities needed to enter sacred space. The ultimate purpose of a sacred site is to allow participants to encounter the sacred.

To create sacred place or space, history is imperative. It may be the storied history already present in the physical matter of a place, or it may be history we find in our research about a particular site. We may also use information from history to locate and then re-create an assemblage of the natural elements used at sacred sites throughout time (stone, water, nature, music, words, sacraments, visuals). At least some of these elements are required in creating or re-creating sacred sites.

Additionally, we must relate the new sacred site to spirit-rituals that will create a community of people of like minds and purposes. We must honor God with the site—how it is built, how it sits within nature or its space, the type of activities that take place at the site. We must ask for the blessings of God for purposeful intent. We must create a site where place and space join together visually through the inward and outward flow of nature or appropriate representations of nature. We must include the sensory elements needed to prick the heart of man so that he can acknowledge his need for the sacred. We must create opportunities for feelings and emotions to arise that prepare the spirit, soul, mind, and body for a sacred encounter. And the atmosphere of the site must offer portholes of thin-space for entry into sacred space, usually by offering a sense of contentment, peace, shelter, and solitude if needed.

Connecting with Sacred Sites

According to art historian and professor James Elkins (1997) the major reason we do not personally encounter the sacred in a place or space is the result of our self-centered desires. We do not perceive what is present because we are so focused on what we desire or what we expect.

Sometimes we can try too hard to connect with the sacred power of a site. We attempt to force an encounter, which never works. Or maybe we are simply unprepared or un-ready for a sacred experience. We miss the sacred that may be there with us, and waiting for us, in our attempts to pre-determine or control what occurs.

The crucial factor in a sacred site connection is to create an active human relationship with the holy. There may be access to storied memory or a holy presence, but without human contact and connectivity, the power of a sacred site remains unrevealed. We only connect when the physical properties and the spiritual properties of our human existence join together with the properties of the sacred site.

With What or With Whom do we Connect at Sacred Sites

- **Personal Cognitive Memory:** memory recalled to us by being present at a place or space in the past.
- **Storied Memory:** memory held in the matter of a place, space, or atmosphere waiting to share its story.
- **A Presence:** a presence by God, God's Spirit, or God's messengers—angels.

Chapter 17

- **Spiritual Energy from Creation:** energy presented by the spiritual essence of God's creation—the spirit, soul, or spiritual essence of man and nature.
- **Spiritual Energy:** energy stored or flowing through words, music, art.
- **In-Spirit:** a connection with our personal spirit or an in-spirit connection with another person.

These connections then provide us with

- inspiration or spiritual pondering;
- innovative ideas, words, and thoughts;
- clarity in or for matters already in our minds or spirits;
- direction and advice on things we need to do;
- divine expression or words directly from God;
- a sense of solitude, silence, peace, and reverence;
- a sense of purpose; and/or
- a renewed energy.

In my years of researching the subject of sacred place and sacred space, I have come to understand the importance of these sites in the healing process of the human spirit, soul, mind, and body. We tend to use sacred places and spaces for rote-ritual or traveling destinations, yet they hold a far greater gift. Within the sacred sites of our local community, our state, our country, and our world, there are boundless resources of information and opportunities for sacred enchantment, all simply waiting for us to participate. In our journey into the mystery of a sacred site, we encounter the phenomena of the sacredness of place and space. We find our place in this world and in the next.

Entering the Sacred Space of Sacred Place

Knowledge can tell us about a sacred place, but it cannot lead us within. We are drawn to this place because of its mystery and our imagination. We go there in-body, to a place that has structure, but it is not always the physical structure of a building. It may be a church, a cathedral, an ancient ruin; it may be a porch, the beach, the mountains; or it may be the structure of a book, a musical piece, or an object of art.

Something at this sacred place offers us a gift of enchantment. This enchantment is "the Irish thin-space." The physical sensory stimulation develops into spiritual sensory awareness. We enter the thin-space, transcend from a physical state of being into a meta-physical state of being, and our expanded imagination is unleashed. We are *in-spirit*. We have entered the flow of uninterrupted space. We have entered the sacred space of the sacred place.

Chapter 17

The White Crow's Enchanted Dance

Chapter Eighteen
The White Crow's Enchanted Dance

I had not yet prepared an ending for this book. Somehow, I knew when the time was right, the ending would come. On my last day of editing the text, as I was typing on my back porch—one of my favorite sacred-space places to write—I heard the cawing of a crow. I hear crows most every morning when writing, so this was not an un-familiar occurrence.

I was focused on finishing the last chapter edits, so it took a few seconds for the cawing to capture my full attention. Something about the call seemed persistent. When I finally looked up there was a white crow perched on a branch of the tree beside the porch, just a few feet from where I was sitting!

I have never seen a white crow before. I shut and opened my eyes several times. The crow was still there, all white but for a hood of chestnut brown on the crown of his head and a softer brown on his outer wings and tail. He was talking and dancing, the tree limb swaying under his weight. Before I could think how to respond, he flew away.

As I had done twenty years ago in Cherokee when I first witnessed the enchanted dance of a crow, I walked over to his former dance ground and searched for a feather. None was to be found.

I would like to believe this was the same crow, his feathers, just like my hair, now whitened with age. Or perhaps he was a direct descendent of that Cherokee crow, coming to tell me my story was complete. Or maybe an Irish Hooded Crow asking me to return for a visit. Whatever the case, I took his advice and completed the book that very night. And I am heading to Ireland to release my book this summer, 2017. What better place to end, than as I began. In a sacred place, in sacred space, enchanted by the dance of an enchanted crow!

Chapter 18

The End

Bibliography

Abbey Leix Anthology, Volume One (2010). Franklin, TN: O'More Publishing.

Bachelard, Gaston (1994). *The Poetics of Space: The Classic Look at How we Experience Intimate Places.* Boston, MA: Beacon Books.

Barrie, Thomas (1996). *Sacred Path, Sacred Place: Myth, Ritual, and Meaning in Architecture.* Boston, MA: Shambhala.

Bear Heart (1998). *The Wind is My Mother: The Life and Teaching of a Native American Shaman.* New York: Berkley Books.

Bourke, Vernon, J. (1968). *The Pocket Aquinas.* New York: Washington Press.

Campbell, Anthony (2000) *Margaret Laski's Ecstasy: A Study of Some Secular and Religious Experiences.* Book Review by Anthony Campbell.

Campbell, Joseph (1998). *The Power of Myth—with Bill Moyers.* New York: Doubleday.

Casey, E.S. (1993, 2009). *Getting Back into Place: Toward a Renewed Understanding of the Place-World.* Blooming, IN: Indiana University Press.

Chambers, Oswald (1995). *My Utmost for His Highest.* Edited by James Reimann. Grand Rapids, MI: Discovery House Publishing.

Day, Christopher (2004). *Places of the Soul: Architecture and Environmental Design as a Healing Art,* Second Edition. London: Architectural Press.

Designed for Worship: An Architectural Perspective of Sacred Places in Middle Tennessee. Nashville, TN: The Booksmith Group.

Elkins, James (1997). *The Object Stares Back: On the Nature of Seeing.* Boston, MA: Mariner Books.

Feehan, John (ND). *The Sacredness of Place* article. Dublin: University College Dublin.

Feehan, John (2003). *Farming in Ireland: History, Heritage and Environment*. Tipperary, Ireland: Walsh Printers.

Feehan, John (2010). *The Singing Heart of the World: Creation, Evolution and Faith*. Dublin, Ireland: Columba Press.

Flew, Antony (1979). *A Dictionary of Philosophy*. New York: St. Martin's Press.

Frank, Joseph, Editor (1992). *Sacred Sites: A Guidebook to Sacred Centers & Mysterious Places in the United States*. St. Paul, MI: Llewelynn Publications.

Genzmer, Herbert (2010). *100 Sacred Places: A Discovery of the World's Most Revered Holy Sites*. New York: Parragon.

Hill, Ruth Beebe (1979). *Hanta Yo*. New York: Warner Books.

Hilliard, K. Mark (1998). *An Instructor's Guide to Traditional Native American Games of the Eastern Band of the Cherokee: Grades 5-8*. Dissertation, Middle Tennessee State University, Murfreesboro, TN.

Hilliard, K. Mark (2002). *The Catcher of Dreams: A Wholistic Approach to Wellness Therapy*. Franklin, TN: O'More Publishing.

Hilliard, K. Mark (2006). *Spirit-Ritual: Exploring Spirituality Beyond the Sacred Veil*. Franklin, TN. O'More Publishing.

Hilliard, K. Mark (2008). *Educational Wellness: A Wholistic Approach to the Art and Science of Teaching and Learning*. Franklin, TN: O'More Publishing.

Hilliard, Jack, Hilliard, K. Mark, & Sexton, Jessa (2012). *Proverbs Through the Generations*. Franklin, TN: Hilliard Press.

Hind, Rebecca (2007). *Sacred Places: Sites of Spirituality and Faith*. London: Carlton Books Ltd.

Jay, Roni (1999). *Gardens of the Spirit: Create Your Own Sacred Spaces*. New York: Sterling Publishing Company Inc.

Jung, Carl (1959). *The Undiscovered Self*. New York: New American Library.

Laski, Margaret 1961. *Ecstasy*. London: Cresset Press.

Lehew, Calvin (2003). *Metaphysics 101: Manifesting Your Dreams*. Franklin, TN: Greysmith Publishing, Inc.

Mails, Thomas (1988). *Secret Native American Pathways: A Guide to Inner Peace*. Tulsa, OK: Council Oak Books.

Milne, Courtney (1995). *Sacred Places in North America: A Journey into the Medicine Wheel*. New York: Steward, Tabori, & Chang.

Morozova, Anastasia & Hilliard, K. Mark (2016). *Global Competency: A Guide to Global and Cultural Training for Students, Teachers, Leaders, Businesses, and World Explorers*. Franklin, TN: Hilliard Press

Neihard, John (1932). *Black Elk Speaks*. New York: William Morrow & Company

New American Standard Bible (1999). Grand Rapids, MI: Zondervan Publishing House.

North, P. & North J. (2007). *Sacred Space: House of God, Gate of Heaven*. New York: Continuum.

O'Brien, Kevin (ND). *Clonkeen: Cluain Chaoin–The Beautiful Meadow*. Abbeyleix, Ireland: Abbeyleix Heritage House.

O'Brien, Kevin (1998). *Abbeyleix: Life Lore & Legend*. Abbeyleix, Ireland: Franamanagh Books.

Octavius Brooks Frothingham (1876). *Transcendentalism in New England: A History (1876)*. New York: G.P Putnam's Sons.

O'Donohue, John (1998) *Anam Cara: A Book of Celtic Wisdom*. London: Bantam Press

O'Donohue, John (2004). *Divine Beauty: The Invisible Embrace*. London: Bantam Books.

Packer, Barbara (2007). *The Transcendentalists*. Atlanta, GA: The University of Georgia Press.

Peck, Scott (1978). *The Road Less Traveled: A New Psychology of Love, Traditional Values, and Spiritual Growth*. New York: Simon and Schuster.

Plato (1942). *Five Great Dialogues*. Translated by B. Jowett, Edited by Louise Roper Loomis. New York: The Classics Club.

Richards, Julian (2005). *Stonehenge*. London: English Heritage.

Rogers, William (1947). *Transcendentalism: Truly Remarkable*. Boston, MA: The Christopher Publishing House.

Sexton, Jessa (2016). *Stories of Enchantment: Twelve Fairy Tale Sonnets*. Franklin, TN: Hilliard Press.

Silf, Margaret (2001). *Sacred Spaces: Stations on a Celtic Way*. Brewster, MA: Paraclete Press.

Smith, Huston (1991). *The World's Religions*. New York: Harper Collins Publishers, Inc.

Swan, James. A. (1990). *Sacred Places: How the Living Earth Seeks Our Friendship*. Sante Fe, New Mexico: Bear & Company Publishing.

Thoreau, Henry David (1995). *Walking*. London: Penguin Books.

Walsh, Roger (1990), *Essential Spirituality: The 7 Central Practices to Awaken Heart and Mind*. New York: John Wiley & Sons, Inc.

Wynn, Mark (2009). *Faith in Place: An Essay in Embodied Religious Epistemology*, Oxford, England: Oxford Scholarship Online.

Young, Malcolm C. (2009). *The Spiritual Journal of Henry David Thoreau*. Macon, GA: Mercer University Press.

About the Author and Photojournalist

Dr. K. Mark Hilliard, Author

Dr. Mark Hilliard grew up in a home that was active in daily Bible and Christian studies and practice. At an early age, he began to work alongside his parents who were Christian missionaries serving in small mission communities, including the Appalachian Mountains of East Tennessee and the Eastern Band of the Cherokee Indian Reservation in North Carolina.

Hilliard completed his bachelor's degree from Freed-Hardeman University, majoring in Community Health and Wellness; his Master of Science in Health and Wellness from Middle Tennessee State University; and his Doctor of Arts from Middle Tennessee State University, with an emphasis in higher education and a specialization in health, wellness, and human performance. The majority of his research centered on the physiological, psychological, and spiritual bases for human activity and learning. Professor Hilliard conducted his doctoral dissertation on the Qualla Boundary of the Cherokee

Indian Reservation, with extensive research into the traditional holistic learning styles of the Eastern Band of the Cherokee Indian.

Hilliard devoted his thirty-year career to non-profit education, first in medical education with the American Cancer Society, then in university teaching, research, and administration with several colleges and universities—Columbia State Community College, Middle Tennessee State University, Belmont University, and O'More College of Design. He retired as the president of O'More College in 2014, where he was a distinguished professor of behavioral science and education. Over his career, he taught courses on sacred place and space; spirituality; spirit-ritual; wellness; sensory teaching and learning; global competency; organizational leadership; marriage and family; biophilia; science, myth, and Indian lore; and Cherokee culture.

During his tenure as a college president and professor, Dr. Hilliard oversaw the *President's Society of Fellows and Scholars*; founded and directed the college's *Sensory Teaching and Learning Center*; and founded and directed a student research academy which investigated the concept of sacred place and space. For three years, this experiential learning academy visited sacred sites and conducted interviews with people who had personal stories of sacred place and sacred space experiences. Hilliard also oversaw a cultural field college that included multiple student travel courses to Ireland and the Eastern Band of the Cherokee Indian Reservation; a literary study in New England, including an analysis of Transcendentalism and writings by Ralph Waldo Emerson and Henry David Thoreau; and a study course of Hemingway held in Chicago.

Dr. Hilliard's research academy and field college also took him to England, where he was a member of the Summer Research Institute at Harris Manchester College, University of Oxford, where for four summers he conducted research for his books.

After retirement, Dr. Hilliard established the *Hilliard Institute for Educational Wellness*, a non-profit academic and philanthropic organization. The Institute offers educational workshops on sensory teaching and learning, workshops and courses on sacred place and space, and fundraising activities in support of select individual and small non-profit organization needs. Most recent projects include raising money to build a well in Haiti, the funding to build a village school kitchen in Uganda, and continued yearly support of a Christian mission program on the Eastern Band of the Cherokee Indian Reservation. The Institute's newest project is the release of this book and a two-week summer course on sacred place and sacred space in Abbeyleix, Ireland, Summer 2017.

Emily Mae Bergeron, Photojournalist

Emily Mae Bergeron is a Tennessee-based photographer and photojournalist for the Hilliard Institute and Moloney-O'Brien Publishing. She enjoys traveling and being in nature. In her professional career and travels, she has shot throughout Ireland, France, Italy, and the United States with many more destinations on her bucket list.

When asked about being the photojournalist for *The Crow's Enchanted Dance* Emily readily agreed. The book is an apt project for Emily who explains, "I strive to tell a story through my photos. I want those who view my work to feel that they are transported and immersed in what they see. I enjoy capturing the beauty of a moment for others to experience."

Live in the Wonder of God

by Jessa Rose Sexton

"Holy, holy, holy is the Lord Al-
mighty: all the earth is full of His glory."
Call me then into your presence—enthrall
me with the awesomeness of your story.

Why does dullness pervade my days? Surround-
ed by the evercasting light of the
Everlasting Might of my God—dumbfound-
ed should be my response: not complacency.

But blindness to beauty becomes simple.
Too simple—why? When the Maker of those
marvelous stars (all those stars!), is mindful
of me—in my frozen phase, I'm still chos-
en—why can't I live in the wonder of
God, when all earth is a sight of His love?

Isaiah 6:3

www.ingramcontent.com/pod-product-compliance
Lightning Source LLC
Chambersburg PA
CBHW042320150426

43192CB00001B/2